EDIT YOUR WAY

SELF-EDITING ESSENTIALS TO KNOW BEFORE EVER TOUCHING A COMMA

ANGELA JAMES

For information about bulk ordering discounts, special discounts for educational classrooms, or to obtain permission to use snippets from this book, please contact Angela James LLC at support@angelajames.co

Visit the author's website at angelajames.co

This book was always going to have to be dedicated to my husband, who's listened to me talk about Before You Hit Send for over fifteen years and who will tell anyone and everyone that he's my biggest fan. And he lives that truth every day.
I love you, JJW.

CONTENTS

NOTE ABOUT AI

If anyone accuses this book of being written by AI, I'll probably fall off my chair laughing because 1) *at least* 50% of this book was written over a decade ago and 2) AI has a better ability to form logical sentences than I do. I don't think anyone would ask AI to write in ADHD, lol.

And you can pry my em dashes from me…never.

RESOURCES
IN THIS BOOK

Throughout this book, I mention a number of different social media posts, articles, and books that you may wish to read.

I also make note of a variety of free downloads, products, and workshops I offer.

If you'd like to interact with any of these resources, I've provided a list of everything that I've referenced on my website at angelajames.co/resources

If you have any questions about these resources, please contact us at support@angelajames.co

AUTHOR'S NOTE

Before You Hit Send® started as a one-week course in 2010, evolved into a four-week course and has been a work in progress since I held that first iteration.

The language and terms that we use have evolved in that time. But what's particularly changed is the understanding of how harmful some language can be, and what microaggressions look like. Though I refreshed the course in 2019 to remove harmful and problematic language, some things still went unnoticed until 2021, when I again refreshed, changed even more things, and then had it professionally proofread.

Then, of course, I again revised as I turned the course lessons into this book, and I hired an expert in DEI to review the language used as well as individual lessons, and again had it professionally proofread (twice).

I'm grateful to everyone who's worked on this content with me over the years, and anything that remains that has not been changed/revised I take full responsibility for.

If there is anything you feel needs to be brought to my attention for further review and revision, I always welcome feedback and new insight, as I, and my team, learn and grow. As we know better, we will always strive to do better.

You can email me and my team at support@angela-james.co

~Angela

SECTION ONE
BUILDING YOUR EDITING FOUNDATION

CHAPTER 1
WHY EDITING SUCKS
BUT IS IMPORTANT

There is nothing sexy about editing a book. Yes, I'm an editor, I should be all "rah-rah, editing rocks!" right? But no. I mean, don't get me wrong, I love editing, of course I do, but I realize not everyone does and I totally understand why.

Now, writing a book? That can come with a certain mystique, a sense of cachet, a feeling of celebration when you type, even just metaphorically, "The End". People celebrate you when you finish writing a book and get that first draft done. Those who have written a book know that feeling of elation when you've gotten through the first draft. Those who haven't written a book find it awe-inspiring and often have all sorts of questions about the process.

But there's no one that says "oooh, you edited your book? That's amazing! How did you do it?"

Editing a book just isn't sexy. And it's *because* I'm an editor that I can say that.

But you know what editing is? It's rewarding. And

I'm not just talking about intangibly rewarding. I mean rewarding in a way that creates actual, tangible results.

EDITING IS REWARDING

Editing is rewarding because it can further connect you, the author, to the story and the characters.

And even more importantly, it can connect *the reader* to the story and characters.

When you edit, you turn your attention from the story you've been driven to write, to the story the readers are reading. You move from thinking inward, to thinking outward. In editing, you think less of "what I want and what the characters demand" and you start thinking more about the reader experience.

The reader experience is the ultimate goal of editing. It's the underpinning of the choices you make as you attempt to shape the final version of the book into something that readers will love, gush over, recommend, record TikTok videos about, share on social media, read, re-read, and buy the ebook, the print version and the special edition copy.

And when you connect reader and story, when they can't turn the pages fast enough, that's how you move a reader from a casual reader to someone who says they'll read your grocery list.

Writing "the end" is sexy, but editing for the reader experience leads to the ultimate reward: happy fans.

And creating happy fans is the goal of this series of books.

Because happy fans love what you write, want more of what you write, buy more books, sell more books to other readers on your behalf, and help create more fans. All of those result in the intangible rewards, and the tangible rewards.

Yep, editing is rewarding.

So if you're an author looking for happy fans, or an editor looking for ways to further help your authors get there, welcome! This book is for you!

CHAPTER 2
CREATING EXPECTATIONS

This is a book about how you can have confidence in the editing process and the steps you can take to achieve that.

It's not a "how to fix commas and pacing" manual. That comes in the other books in this series.

Still, don't let that make you think this is a book that's not actionable, because I'm going to share some very practical knowledge:

- I'll talk about the different stages of editing and what to expect in Chapter 9.
- I cover working with editors, critique partners, and beta readers in Chapter 9.
- I'm going to tell you where to start edits (Chapter 11), when to know you're done with edits (Chapter 12), and even give you a suggested workflow for how to approach your edits (Chapter 10).
- There's also a chapter about author voice (Chapter 6)

- And a very important chapter to get you thinking about writing and editing for inclusivity (Chapter 8).

This isn't a book about fixing commas because, above all, this is a book that aims to reduce your editing frustration (not eliminate it because let's be honest, that's impossible) by getting you to a place of understanding *about how to actually move through the editing process itself* so you can start edits, do edits, and end edits in a way that's more efficient, more effective and less "flailing hands and throwing spaghetti".

The most frustration that authors experience with editing usually comes about because they don't know where to start, they don't know how to proceed to be effective, and they don't know when to be done.

In this book, I set you up for editing success by diving into the editing foundations.

I *am* going to tell you how to figure out all of that.

This isn't a one-size-fits-all process, because every author is unique.

Sure, you've heard that before. But then you're expected to follow some arbitrary "rules", follow an exact map of steps, and still come out the other side with a book that stands out in the market.

This book is not a book that wants or expects you to be the same as every other author.

Through this book, I want you to embrace your author voice and your characters' voices. I want you to figure out what writing "rules" are suited to your writing, which ones hinder it and when you should say "eff the writing rules", and I want you to create an editing process that works for you and helps you start, proceed and finish.

I can't make that happen for you, but I can give you the tools to do it. This entire book is your toolbox, and we're going to add to the toolbox throughout the rest of the series!

Read Me!

I know there are some books on writing and editing you can skip around in. But I suggest reading this particular book from front to back because I take you through a series of chapters that parallel the lessons from the *Before You Hit Send®* course and explain how to create your own editing process.

I try to layer the information in a way that creates a build-up in your knowledge and understanding of your own editing process.

I also take a pretty good whack at answering the questions people who are new to editing or those authors struggling with editing have, including where to start, where to end and how to create an editing checklist.

If you read from front to back, engage with the exercises and give yourself some time and space to do so, you will have your editing process ready for your next edit.

I know some of you aren't linear readers, and will want to skip around, and that's totally fine! At the back of the book, as an addendum, I've provided a few "roadmaps" through this book. One of those roadmaps might appeal to you more if you like to jump around!

Each chapter is a unique lesson, and I've attempted to provide a few things to make them easily digestible and actionable. In the individual chapters, you'll find some combination of these things:

- A TL;DR (Too Long; Didn't Read) to give you an overview of each lesson.
- Action Step(s) to help you implement things within your own manuscripts
- Tips & Tidbits contain additional information about the lessons, using Q&As from past students who've taken the course.
- Additional Resource recommendations or links to further your learning.

Indulge Me! (While I set the stage for you to best utilize this book.)

1. Give yourself space to absorb the content and to apply it to your work.

Part of the editing process, especially once you start working with an editor, is absorbing what your editor, critique partner, or beta reader is suggesting, but it's also an important part of self-editing to not rush through it.

Don't be in a hurry

Rushing the editing process, both in self-edits and with an editor, only results in a less refined product. Slow down and absorb, reread, and do a thorough job.

Deliver the best possible product to your readers by not trying to cut corners and rush the process!

2. Come to this book with an open mind to learning new ways of thinking about concepts and the craft of writing.

Much like approaching edits, approaching this book with a sense of openness and willingness to make changes will allow you to have greater learning and growth throughout the book (and throughout your writing career).

I firmly believe that authors should come from a place of ongoing learning and understand that there's always room to grow their craft, both in the larger scope and in the smaller details.

It's exactly the same for an editor, and I, myself, am always on a journey of learning about the craft of writing, publishing, and marketing.

3. It's totally okay to disagree with me.

Maybe you have firm opinions about adverbs or commas or passive voice. I'm not going to argue you out of those because I want to focus on the positive energy of encouraging your self-confidence in edits, not tear down your opinions.

Writing is perfectly subjective, even in the times when people think something should be a "rule." Not only that, if we all wrote exactly the same, publishing would be a boring place of uniformity and lack creativity. The exact opposite of what publishing is meant to be about.

Plus, when it comes to writing "rules", *there's no one authority on how writing works* (including—especially—

me). There's only advice that you can take or leave as it works for you.

4. You may be wondering if you should do all of the editing yourself or pay for an editor.

This series of books isn't meant as a replacement for hiring editors, but instead is meant as a tool to help you develop the skills to self-edit your own work to a point where you get greater value from the editors you work with, because they can focus on what's needed, rather than trying to fix everything.

I hope I make it clear in this book that there's a tremendous amount of value to be found in working with a good developmental editor, with the *right* developmental editor.

Similarly, working with a solid copy editor and/or proofreader can take your work to the next level of polish and brand quality.

So I'm always going to be Team Hire an Editor. But I also recognize that not everyone is going to do that.

If you're planning on not hiring an editor, I do advise finding someone to barter or swap with to get some feedback, because we can't see what we cannot see in our own work, and getting outside input is invaluable.

But whether you hire an editor or not, this series of books will help you improve your skills, making you a better self-editor than you were before!

CHAPTER 3

ANGELA'S KEY PRINCIPLES OF EDITING AND OTHER IMPORTANT THOUGHTS (THAT'S A JOKE)

Turning *Before You Hit Send*® from a course to a book has been one of the things that's been most requested of me over the past 15 years the course has been in existence. Thousands of students have gone through the course, and some of them have gone through it multiple times, each time with a new goal in mind, and new takeaways they were after. And many of them have asked for a book, hoped for a book, wondered when it would be a book.

My answer was always, "Someday."

At one point, years ago, I thought it was time. I got an agent, created a book proposal, revised a book proposal and then just...sat on it.

It wasn't the right time. I didn't know what I wanted the book to be. I didn't know how to take weeks of course material and turn it into a book.

Truth be told, I also didn't necessarily love the direction I was asked to take the book either. It felt...cold, impersonal, and completely devoid of my personality and voice. As you read this book, you'll know that if there's one thing I think about writing, it's that voice matters.

And if there's one thing I know about *Before You Hit Send*® as a course, and now as a book, it's that my voice matters in every aspect of the lessons.

So you'll find this book is full of my voice and my personality, as well as leaning into my core beliefs about editing.

Because of that, I think that knowing some of my core values around editing (and publishing) might help you figure out if I'm the editor you want to learn from and if this is the book for you.

These are my consistent key principles that you'll see repeated in some form or another, not just through this book, and the other books in the set, but also throughout all my memberships, workshops, and newsletter.

1. Voice is crucial.
2. There are no writing rules.
3. Commas aren't as important as content.
4. Developmental editing is where the magic happens.
5. You don't need an editor but without one, you'll never be as good as you could be.
6. Finding a good editor fit is as important as finding the right best friend.
7. Write for yourself, edit for the reader's experience.
8. Ego is in all of us, don't let it get in the way.
9. Know your brand aka Don't Kill the Dog.

10. You're not writing (or editing) for every
reader.

1. Voice is crucial.

For all fifteen of my years in traditional publishing, and
then in all the years beyond that as an indie editor, I've
found myself training and mentoring dozens of new
editors, and one of the first things I have always taught
is to respect an author's writing voice during the
editing process.

Author voice is what separates compulsively readable stories from tired cliches and familiar storylines. It
gives the characters, plot, story and world-building that
extra zhuzh. And it's the thing that overcomes questionable grammar and craft, to keep the readers hooked.

This book contains a lot of references to author
voice, and that's because it's one of the keystones of
creating reader fans.

2. There are no writing rules.

I can't even remember when I first started using this
sentence, but it's been at least fifteen years. It's a
sentence that grabs attention, but also that authors often
most struggle with for one simple reason: the idea of
writing "rules" can be comforting even when it's frustrating, because at least if there are "rules" there's something objective and easy to implement in edits.

But those writing "rules", as well-intentioned as
they may be, are also most often the villain in the story
of killing an author's voice, creating writer's block and

turning a voice-filled story into something that colors within the lines.

For that reason, I always urge authors (and editors) to look beyond the idea of the absolute "musts" and "shoulds" and "nevers" and instead ask the question: what will the readers' experience be with this book and what are the most important elements to revise.

Hint: it's rarely adverbs. Or commas.

3. Commas aren't as important as content.

This is another key principle that can trip authors up because commas are a lot easier to fix than plot, world-building, pacing, character development and so on. Commas are tangible, there are style guides in place that tell you how commas work, they're little and they don't feel intimidating.

But having well-placed commas isn't going to make a reader fall in love with your story. And a large majority of readers don't care if you're missing well-placed commas either (sorry to those who are passionate about commas, but it's true).

Because what they want is a story that captivates, characters they can love (or hate), and a book that will be worth their time and money. Something they can think about, talk about, and recommend.

Commas aren't that. That's why they'll never be as important as content.

4. Developmental editing (aka content editing, or dev editing) is where the magic happens.

Too many authors skip developmental edits simply because they just don't know how to edit or what that can look like.

Which is truly a shame, because developmental editing is like a magic portal to uplevel your book. It can take a decent read or a good read, to a great read or a transformative read.

It's also where you can learn the most about your writing and apply those learnings to the next book and the next. Also magical!

Some might call me biased, since I'm a developmental editor, but what I am is someone who's experienced and seen the transformative power of developmental edits hundreds of times.

I hope you all will start to fall a little more in love with developmental editing for that reason.

5. You don't need an editor but without one, you'll never be as good as you could be.

Okay, yes, again, I know you probably think I'm biased when I say this, and it does sound like a little bit of hyperbole but…

I do believe that a great editor, who's a good match for your books, with the skills to deliver meaningful story, plot, character, pacing, world-building notes (in other words, developmental edits) can meaningfully and positively impact not just one book, but all subsequent books you write.

I've seen this in action, having had authors come back to me years after working together and tell me this is how it worked for them (as well as mention my positive impact on their work in acceptance speeches and acknowledgments).

What they learned, they were able to apply over and over again. They were able to improve their skills, lean into their author voice, give the reader more and grow into best-selling authors.

That's hard to do when the only voice in your head is your own, because you don't know what you don't know.

Hire the right editor. At least once.

One of my beta readers said, *"I wonder if this might be a good place to include some client testimonials saying just exactly this? An author voice might make the point even more powerfully."* So off I went to my folder of editing testimonials to find something to use. I'm fortunate to have different quotes to choose from but this one, from a discussion in one of my author memberships, seemed to prop up my point beautifully.

 This morning I started a new opening scene for the contemporary romance Angela gave me dev edits on... AND I LOVE IT. Honestly, the feedback was incredible and invaluable, and now I know exactly how to fix a manuscript that was so/so but had potential. I haven't been this excited about writing in a while. Best writing advice I can give… find an editor you trust who can give you the insight you need to move forward with your stories to help improve your craft.

— Edith Lalonde, multi-published author

6. Finding a good editor fit is as important as finding the right best friend.

It hurts me to say that there are bad editors out there but…there are bad editors out there. I don't want to dog on anyone else trying to build their business but, frankly, editing is a skilled job and not everyone who thinks or says they can do it has the skills to do it well, with a meaningful, positive impact on the story and the author.

And, well, not every editor is the right match for you. *I* am not the right editor for every book or author.

I think sometimes finding the best edit match can be harder than dating, because at least in dating, you get to actually, you know, date before making a commitment. That's a lot harder to do when you're hunting for an editor.

Bad experiences happen, and bad editors happen (sorry to say, but bad authors happen to good editors too) and wading through to find the right one can be full of time, pain and, unfortunately, money. This is why I offer products like EditMatch: The Complete Toolkit for Choosing the Right Editor, give advice on finding the right editor in my author communities, and why I wrote parts of this book—to help you avoid the wrong editor, and match with the one who gets you.

It's worth it in the long run, finding the right one who can make magic with you, so don't give up too soon.

7. Write for yourself, edit for the reader's experience.

"I just write what the characters tell me to."

"The story goes where it wants to go and I'm just the vessel."

Writing is a solitary and difficult endeavor. Getting the words on the page can be painful, sometimes ponderous, and feel as if you're only getting a word or two every minute. If that.

Everyone has a different writing style, and a different way of getting that story onto the screen or paper. I think it's important to do what works for you when you're writing, to help the story flow and get that first draft done.

Don't let too many voices of other authors or editors in your head as you're writing, letting that interfere with how you experience the story and the writing.

Write. Just write. Write for yourself, write for your characters, write to get it out.

But then...when it's time to edit, it's time to think about how the reader is going to experience the story. They will never (ever) experience it like you did when writing it, so it's going to be your job to make sure that the story you wanted to tell and meant to tell is the story that's on the page.

That the story gives the reader an escape, an experience, a transport into the book and a journey along with the characters.

Writing is for you. Editing is for the reader.

8. Ego is in all of us, don't let it get in the way.

We all have an ego—some of us have more ego than we should, some of us don't have as much ego as we should.

But when I'm talking about ego in the editing process, it's not just having an "I'm too good for editing" attitude, but also "this is my book baby and no one can tell me how to raise it" plus "I'll do whatever you say because I just want this book to be good and I don't believe in myself" (noooo), and on the editor side, "I'm the expert, you must bow down to me." (lol)

I'm sure many of you have encountered some of these varieties of "ego" before.

When I say that ego can be harmful and detrimental to both the editing process and the publishing process if we don't rein it in, imagine me shaking my head at the idea of someone's ego (whether author's or editor's) entering edits in a way that creates roadblocks to the process, and saying "shew-wha-whoo" (shew-wha-whoo being the sound my best friend makes when someone has disappointed her or is "a lot".)

Dealing with someone else's ego (again, on both sides of the editing process) when you're trying to work as a team on a book is probably one of the hardest things, because you don't want to hurt anyone's feelings, but you also want everyone in the process to be open to change, feedback and discussion. And not only that, but you want them to have enough of an ego about their book to be able to say no, stand up for their book and not make every change suggested.

Letting your ego rule your decisions is a big impediment to positive growth and changes (and not just in edits, lol), and positive growth and change is the entire purpose of editing!

9. Know your brand aka Don't Kill the Dog.

Brand is a huge concept that's fairly misunderstood. For instance, you may not think this book and the rest of the books in this series are outwardly about branding, since I'm specifically talking about editing, but they really *are* also about your author brand.

Most authors think of brand as something visual: colors, logo, font, etc. But that's just one part of your brand (the visual brand part) and honestly the part that comes last because you can't decide the visuals until you know what they represent.

Your brand is your promise to readers.

What they can expect from your books, even when the subgenre or genre might change. Why they can trust spending their money and their time on your books.

It's a combination of voice and storytelling.

And knowing your brand can actually make editing easier, because you'll be able to tell when something fits and when something doesn't.

Understanding your own brand enables you to better understand when killing off a dog, or a beloved character, is going to negatively impact your relationship with your readers, their trust in you, and their willingness to spend time and money on your books.

It can mean that you know you might need to reconsider killing the dog because it's not the right thing for your brand (or your audience).

And, of course, not incidentally, it becomes a whole lot easier to market your books if you understand your brand.

10. You're not writing (or editing) for every reader.

Who is this book for? One of the questions my beta readers and I discussed.

Here's what I know: this book is for you if you're someone who wants to get better at the editing process, who doesn't mind parenthetical thoughts amongst your text, and who is interested in understanding the foundations of editing, not just looking for a fast track to fixing commas. This book is for you if you want to learn the beginning of the editing process, not just the middle and the end.

This book isn't for those of you who get impatient with learning processes, want a magical quick fix for editing (it doesn't exist), and who like the Pittsburgh Penguins (that's a hockey joke).

Join me on the journey?

This book, and the subsequent books in the series, will take you on an editing journey. This one is the foundation that's going to help you understand your own editing process, how to set it up and why you need one. Later books will dive more significantly into how to edit, what exactly to look for, and where you can make the greatest impact.

Why am I telling you this? Because I'm demonstrating the concept of understanding I'm not writing for every reader. I'm writing for the author who needs this book and wants this book.

Something that trips up nearly every author is the question "who do you want to read your book" and they say "everyone".

The answer really isn't everyone. You're not writing your book for everyone, it's not going to appeal to everyone, and oh, by the way, some people are going to hate your voice, your characters, your story, and the way you use punctuation and spell the word "gray".

Being clear on what your readers love in the books they love is going to help you edit the book for their reading experience. Don't worry about the people who aren't going to love it, they're not who you're writing, editing or publishing for.

When I say we're editing for the readers' experience, I don't mean *all* readers, I mean *your* readers. The readers who are looking for the kind of story you're writing.

Just as your book(s) aren't for every reader, I know that mine won't be for every author. That's okay; let's both embrace that!

So there's your overview to *Edit Your Way* and a great look at my writing style, my teaching style and my editing style.

If these 10 things sound like principles of editing

and publishing that work for you, welcome, I'm going to take you on an epic journey of becoming your own best editor!

And for all of you who asked over the years when *Before You Hit Send*® was going to be a book, I have a new answer...

"Today."

CHAPTER 4
QUICK WIN—LISTEN OR READ ALOUD

This lesson has so much value—often unexpected value—that in 2022 I moved it back to the beginning of *Before You Hit Send®*, where it used to reside in early versions of the course. Now, I'm including it as a chapter in this book even though I know it doesn't *quite* belong in *Edit Your Way,* and yet…I feel it needs to be here so you can see an example of what quick wins look like, since I talk about them later in the book.

And also so you can simply get a quick win if you want one.

But perhaps *most importantly*, because it brings you closer to what the readers' experience with your book is, and that's a concept I center on in this book.

Still, I recognize, and you will too, that it is an outlier in this book, in that much of this book is focused on understanding the foundation and processes of editing, rather than specific how-tos (which come in later books in this set). But it's so valuable that I felt I had to include it here! Plus, it gives you a look into what the books that come after this one in the series will look like, with specific, actionable writing and editing skills.

Even if you think you've done this or heard this advice before, it's a valuable tool to revisit and can offer an easy quick win when you're feeling stumped on edits.

To really dig into your manuscript and get more of the reader's experience, you should listen to your manuscript.

TL;DR

- Listening or reading aloud is one of the most effective editing tools you can add to your writing toolkit.
- By doing this you'll read what's on the page, not what you *think* is on the page.
- This gives you a different perspective on your writing.
- Don't edit as you listen! Give yourself a chance to experience the story as a reader and just make notes or annotate the text.

———

As I was working on this book, I met weekly with an accountability partner, my friend Jennie Mustafa-Julock, and during the course of one of those meetings, we were chatting about audiobooks and recording books.

During that conversation, Jennie told me about a previous business book she'd written, *Hilda: Tackle Your*

Inner Naysayer, Get Out of Your Own Way, and Unleash Your Badassery, and how she recorded the audio version of *Hilda* months after it had been published in eBook and print. While recording, she found herself finding typos or areas that she probably could have smoothed out or revised, and ended up saying more than once, "Darnit, why didn't I read this aloud *before* I published the book."

She told me that story first, with no prompting from me, and then I told her that Listening/Reading Aloud was actually a core chapter in the self-editing book. And her experience is exactly why! Because when you listen or read aloud, if you're able, you will become even more aware of what the reader is experiencing as they read.

(And in case anyone is wondering, I did listen to parts of this book, specifically the new sections I added as well as a few other sections such as the one on editing for inclusivity, that were of utmost importance to me to get right!)

LISTEN OR READ ALOUD

This is perhaps the advice I utilize most frequently in workshops and in edits. When I first started teaching editing, the advice I gave was to read aloud, and indeed, that's what you'll still hear from many editors. But over the years, with the advance of technology as well as my realization that reading aloud can still create some barriers, I now recommend that authors listen.

Before I begin, I do want to acknowledge that this isn't a technique that will be accessible to everyone, so I offer below a few different alternate suggestions to try if you're unable to listen to and / or read aloud your work.

LISTEN AND/OR READ ALOUD

I think this is one of the best tips you can get to help with editing, and when I do critiques and edits it's often the one thing I tell everyone to do, because of the sheer value in creating a distance from what you think is on page and what is actually on page.

Let your computer, phone, or some other device read it to you. Listen to the dialogue, the narrative, the blocking (sometimes also called choreography or how you move characters around on page).

How you think the book should sound, how you hear it in your head as you read, is often not what's actually on the paper.

The reason I recommend listening (versus reading aloud) is because listening takes you totally outside your own head, takes out the inflections you think should be there and gives you a completely impersonal reading of the book. It also prevents you from still filling in what you think should be there—or how you think it should sound—and instead reads to you only what's on the page. It gives you a better idea of the readers' experience with your story.

The computer doesn't infer any emotion, and has no

emphasis, and doesn't do anything except read the words exactly as they are on the page. This forces you to process the story more as a reader would, coming to it without being within your head and your understanding of the book.

When you listen to your book read aloud, you're removing some of your own filtered experience (expectations of what's on the page) and creating for yourself more of the reader's experience (versus the author's experience).

Why Should You Listen or Read Aloud?

Because it allows you to gain a distance from your own work.

Which then allows you to:

1. Hear where your narrative and dialogue aren't working.
2. Understand where/how/why story structure isn't working.
3. Note where you've left out a word or used the wrong one.
4. Realize where you've written description or dialogue that is going to make your readers snicker.
5. Understand where you've got awkward or unnatural dialogue between your characters, or where someone sounds too formal or stilted.
6. See repetitive sentence structure or word usage.

7. Discover where you've inserted too much backstory, info dumping, or started in the wrong place.
8. See where you've left out description, confused your reader, or inserted too much blocking.
9. Figure out where you've bored even yourself!

If you ask me if a passage, sentence, or piece of dialogue sounds right, the first thing I'm going to ask you is if you listened to it. Listening moves you outside of your own head and gives you a bit of distance from the work. I'll bet anyone who's heard their work in audiobook format (or done a live reading of their work) can agree!

If you don't have time to set a manuscript or edits aside for a few days or weeks, then listening is the best way to get some distance and hear what's really there instead of what you think is there.

You know why else you should listen to your work?

Because it's a wonderful opportunity to fall in love with your own writing and storytelling. Yes, you might be a little embarrassed to listen at first, but so many authors have told me after listening to their books that they realized how much they actually really like their writing, loved the story, and how it wasn't as terrible as they'd convinced themselves it was.

Listen to your story not just for the things that need

work, but for the parts that are great, fantastic even, and for the things you do well.

Listen for the lines that catch your attention (those might be marketing quotes!), the dialogue that flows wonderfully, and the scenes that are just *chef's kiss* perfection.

In other words, don't think you have to be only critical of your work as you listen. Take the time to be proud of yourself and to really enjoy your writing.

When to implement this practice

There's no one right time in the writing process for this technique. Instead, it's more along the lines of…when you need it and when you're ready for it.

Usually, it's going to happen after you've written at least an initial draft, but here are some recommendations for when to listen.

- When you're stuck or struggling with a scene, have a creative block or don't know how to "fix" something.
- At a point when you want to process the story more from the readers' perspective and gain more insight about what's actually on the page versus what you think you wrote.
- Before sending the book to beta readers or proofreaders, when you're still in the initial edits stage.
- After you've received feedback and you're not sure about the feedback, need to process

the feedback or want to get some ideas about what your readers experienced.

- Any time you want to remind yourself why a scene works, or what is great about your writing, and that no, you don't suck. Stop telling yourself you suck and no one wants to read your book. There's a reader waiting for your book!

Deep Breath...

Don't be self-conscious about listening and/or reading aloud.

If you need to, find a quiet spot away from your family and begin reading aloud or pop in some earphones and let the computer read to you. Think of it as practice for when your book becomes an audiobook.

How is it going to sound to the people listening to it on their treadmills, or in their cars on their way to work? How much will your sight-impaired readers enjoy hearing it rather than seeing it?

Get comfortable with the act of reading aloud or listening. You may even wish to tape yourself reading it aloud so you can play it back.

Text to Speech Apps

A few free options, depending on whether you're a PC or Mac user:

- If you use Word, right-click in your document and select "Read Aloud".

- If you use Pages on Mac, just right-click in your document and select "Speech, start speaking".
- If you're using Google Docs, you will need to do some research into this because at the time of this book, there isn't an easy way to do this, except by downloading extensions.
- If you use Scrivener, there is also a text-to-speech option in the menu which is called "Start Speaking".
- Natural Reader (PC)
- Speechify
- Another option if you own an e-reader is loading the manuscript onto your e-reader. Some Kindle versions have this option (the actual e-reader, not the Kindle program on another device), and there may be other devices that do as well.
- There are also several app options on both Android and iPhone platforms that now do text to speech. You may particularly want to search for PDF-to-speech apps, if you'd like a phone app for this.

Get Started

How *you* use listening or reading aloud as a tool in *your* editing is individual, so there's no right or wrong way to do it, but I have a few suggestions to help you get started:

1. Edit in chunks. Don't feel you need to sit down and read the whole book aloud. Try this:

- Start at the beginning and listen to the first chapter.
- Do a sample of the manuscript in the middle where a "saggy middle" can bog a manuscript down.
- Identify the sections that have been giving you trouble.
- Listen to the last few chapters to see how the finale will read.
- Read a few random pages, a random scene, or a random chapter. You don't need to read the whole book aloud (unless you want to!).

2. Look at this as a way to get a sense of the flow of your writing, both narrative and in dialogue. Often if you pick up trouble spots in one area, you'll be able to extrapolate that to the whole book.

3. Don't edit as you listen. Decide on a system of flagging while you're listening. Highlighting the area, a quick comment, etc. Don't stop to edit each time you hear something. Instead, flag it to come back to. Stopping to edit each time prevents you from hearing the scene as a whole and getting in the flow of the book as a reader would.

4. Take note of the places you stop or something that catches your attention (both good and bad).
If you find a certain word or phrase pops out, it may be a place that readers pause as well. Do you want them to pause here?

5. Pay attention to how much attention you're paying.
Are you drifting off, losing focus, getting bored or impatient to get to the good stuff as you're listening to your own manuscript? This may be a sign you've started in the wrong place, got the pacing wrong, or have too much info dump/backstory.

6. Accommodate for your own needs.
Of course, getting bored or attention drifting off could also mean that you're like me and have ADHD or are otherwise neurodivergent, or have difficulty with audio processing, so you may need to find ways to keep your own attention:

- My personal favorite is finding a way to listen at a higher speed (anywhere from 1.7 to 2.0 speed is my preferred speed for audiobooks, podcasts and videos).
- Other ideas are to listen in much smaller chunks, read aloud instead of listening, or take more in-depth notes while you're listening to stay engaged.

7. Listen to areas that you love and aren't trouble areas.

We focus so much on the negative or on the criticism, that sometimes we forget that also understanding what we do well is also important. Listen to those lines and story parts that just have great story, flow, character interaction, dialogue, action. Why are they great? How can you apply that to other areas of the manuscript?

8. Pay attention to great lines or sections that you can use for marketing.

Authors often struggle to find great marketing quotes once the book is written because they didn't mark or highlight areas while in the trenches of writing and editing. By marking areas while you're listening (and editing in general), you'll be saving time and energy that you won't have to replicate again, and your future self will thank you for doing that work.

Additional options other than listening/reading

If listening or reading aloud isn't an option, here are a few other ideas you can try to get a more outside perspective of your work in progress:

1. Take a break from the manuscript. Taking time away from your manuscript after typing The End is something that provides distance between you and the story.

Giving your brain time to come out of being immersed in the world and the words on the page offers an opportunity to re-examine the story with a fresh perspective.

When you do this, you have a better chance of critiquing what's there and understanding what's missing. It's an opportunity to move from what your brain believes it wrote and what's actually on the page.

You may see missing details, uneven plot threads, shallow characterization and more with some time and distance from the story.

A few days is good, but a few weeks is much better!

2. Give your brain space to wander and be creative. Some people may use the expression "let yourself be bored" but sometimes when I'm bored, that's all I can think about. Instead, don't try to fill your brain twenty-four seven.

When your mind is given downtime that doesn't require it to be actively engaged is when creative inspiration, new ideas and block breakthroughs can happen.

Let your mind wander around your story while you're:

- Exercising—on the treadmill, at the gym, practicing yoga.
- In the shower—your brain doesn't need to focus on washing your body, that's automatic, so there's room for creativity.
- Doing household chores such as dishes, cleaning off your desk, shoveling snow.
- Driving in the car, running errands.

- Outside in the yard or other outdoor spaces.
- In bed, relaxing, falling asleep.

The idea here is to give your brain space. For you, that may mean not playing podcasts or listening to music. Or it may mean that you need to engage part of your brain with something like music in order to let the other part wander.

How this works is going to look different for everyone. For instance, I get a lot of inspiration in the shower where everything is a bit mindless, with no other background noise happening. But when I'm walking the dogs, I get more inspiration if I have a business podcast on to jumpstart my creative thoughts.

Pay attention to when your creative breakthroughs seem to come, and try to plan to let yourself have more time in those spaces.

AND THIS IS CRUCIAL!!

Make sure you have some way to get your creative breakthroughs written down or recorded somehow.

The worst part of letting your brain wander and

having a breakthrough is when you later forget it because you think "Oh, I'll remember."

You won't remember, lol. We've all done that on the edge of sleep or in the shower, amirite?

3. Do a readthrough of the manuscript on different platforms/mediums or using a different font. For instance, if you write on your laptop, read your manuscript on your phone or on an e-reader. Or print out pages and edit on paper. Alternately, change the font in your document to something different.

Looking at the book on different screens or in a unique way gives your brain a different way of seeing what's there / what's not.

As an example, I generally do first round developmental edit passes by reading on my Kindle, and then do second round content and line edits on my laptop.

4. Change locations. Changing where you write, edit, or read your work can trip your brain to see things differently much like reading on different platforms or giving yourself time away from the manuscript.

5. Utilize critique partners, beta readers, or editors. An outside viewpoint may give you a whole new perspective!

TAKE ACTION

Your first action step is to listen to the first chapter of your book. Make notes of what you hear and notice about your writing or story, and any realizations you have as you listen.

Following on from this I want you to pinpoint a particular trouble spot in your manuscript, wherever that may be. Take note of where it is, what it is, and what's troubling you about it. *Listen to that area* and make notes about what you notice now. Don't make any changes yet (this is going to be hard!)—just write down what you notice on a sticky note, a piece of paper or in an editing notebook.

I challenge you not to skip this lesson's Take Action steps, even if you think you'll never use listening or reading aloud as an editing tool. Try it just for the experience of it one time. Or if you haven't tried it in a while, do it again with this lesson's information and suggestions in mind.

And you never know: someday you may be doing public readings, so you may as well get comfortable reading your work aloud and hearing it now! If you have read your work aloud yourself in the past, this time let the computer or another program read it to you.

TIPS & TIDBITS

Author Question: When I have the robo-voice read back my work and also have the "track changes" function running, the robo-voice says the crossed-out words instead of the final version. How can I remedy that without turning off the "track changes"?

Angela's Response: If you're in Word, you can view your document in several ways. If you see the tracked changes, you're viewing as "Final Showing Markup" which is the way I generally suggest viewing it. However, if you view as "Final" then you can have it read to you without it reading the crossed-out words. Just be careful to remember you're viewing it like that, before sending it to someone with tracked changes still in it, not realizing you've done that. (You would be sad to know how often authors accidentally query manuscripts with tracked changes in it because of viewing it as "Final".) You might also find it helpful to view the deleted changes in balloons instead of inline. I prefer to view changes in the balloons, as it provides an easier reading experience for me. You could also try that.

ADDITIONAL RESOURCES

If you're curious about hearing more about the "brain space" technique I referred to, we've linked to a short presentation I did about this for a summit/online conference. The video is called *Find Your Creative Space: Finding Your Creativity Among the Chaos of a Busy Brain* and is about 20 minutes on the topic, sharing how this works and ideas for utilizing different techniques to give your brain space. You can find the link to the video on the *Edit Your Way Resources* page on my website angelajames.co.

CHAPTER 5
THE EMOTIONAL JOURNEY OF EDITING

There are a lot of conversations that center around the amount of time and energy—physical and mental—that editing involves, but I'm not sure we spend enough time acknowledging the emotional journey editing can take us on.

In publishing, there sometimes seems to be an expectation that writing a book should and can be approached with a practical, almost distant eye. Even in this book, I often take a very practical approach to edits, making it seem as if editing is always an objective endeavor.

But in reality, very few authors start out thinking—or even end up ever thinking—of their writing and their books as business ventures, and instead have a tremendous emotional investment in their stories, from creation to publication and beyond.

Understanding and acknowledging this emotional investment is a major part of being able to effectively take critique and perform edits, whether that critique is from yourself or an outside source.

On the flip side, sometimes our emotions can cause us to be overly critical, one might say hypercritical, of our work and our stories, and also act as an impediment to effective, useful editing.

So this chapter is focused on emotional awareness, because understanding some of the facts behind our feelings can help make them more manageable. And managing our emotions is an important step in the writing, editing and publishing process.

Typical Emotional Challenges

> *"This manuscript is crap."*
> *"No one is going to want to read this."*
> *"I suck."*
> *"Everything about this story sucks."*
> *"I can't do this."*
> *"Why am I bothering, no editor/agent/reader is going to like this."*
> *"This is a waste of my time."*
> *"I have no idea what I'm doing."*
> *"Ugh."*
> *"I'm going to get awful reviews."*
> *"Everyone hates my writing."*
> *"This manuscript needs to go in the garbage bin because it's beyond saving."*

Any of those sound familiar? Like maybe you heard them recently from your own worst inner critic?

These are all emotional responses to situational stress, and specifically the stress of both writing and editing. When you hit a hurdle, a roadblock or a blank space, and maybe it feels impossible to move forward, and that inner voice kicks in and confirms or amplifies all your worst fears, it becomes even harder to do the thing.

Say hello to imposter syndrome, overwhelm, self-doubt, perfectionism, fear of criticism, fear of/feelings of rejection, feelings of loneliness, and an urge to compare yourself to what everyone else around you is doing.

This is a list of some of what I've found over the past two decades of editing and mentoring authors to be some of the most prevalent and destructive emotions that derail authors from their writing and editing goals.

Self-Doubt: Questioning basically…everything about your writing, your publishing, your creativity. Wondering if you can really do this whole writing thing

Fear of Criticism: Being unable to cope with the idea that people are going to be critical of your thing, whether during writing, during edits, during the querying process or once it's published.

Perfectionism: Believing that you can create some mythical version of a "flawless" manuscript, fix everything that's wrong, and endlessly change and fiddle with things instead of letting it go.

Imposter Syndrome: Thinking things like: you're a fraud, you're not good enough, and you don't deserve to be an author.

Overwhelm: When things just feel like too much, as if you can't possibly do it or handle it, not knowing how to tackle it and just simply feeling as if it's impossible.

Comparison to Others: You know what this is. Stop it. Comparison really is the thief of joy, the creator of imposter syndrome, and the cause of writer's block, self-doubt and perfectionism.

Loneliness: Writing can feel isolating since it's not generally a team sport, unless you're writing with a partner. It feels as if you're doing it all yourself, there's no one to lean on, and you don't have the right support system.

Fear of Rejection: Being convinced that the answer to your question is always going to be "no" whether it's asking an agent to represent you, a publisher to publish you or a reader to read you. Thinking that hearing "no" is the worst possible thing that can ever happen to you and letting it stop you from moving forward.

When do these emotions become a problem?

All of these feelings, emotions and fears can lead to different challenges that create roadblocks in moving forward with your writing and publishing. Here are four of the most common:

Creative Burnout: Creative burnout is an accumulation of things, including ongoing and sometimes seemingly unrelenting intense emotions, trying to do too much too quickly, not giving yourself breaks and rest, and ignoring the mental and physical signs.

I coach authors through all of these, but burnout is often the one I'm most concerned about, because once you reach creative burnout, it's a lot more difficult to bounce back into normal writing routines. And burnout can last anywhere from days to years (yes, years) so it's something I really caution my authors to be alert against.

Avoidance: Generally avoiding writing-and-publishing-related tasks, and it's especially an apparent problem when you're avoiding things you used to love and enjoy, or you're avoiding to the point of never being able to complete/finish anything.

Incompletionism: Starting but never finishing. All your projects. All the half written ones on your hard drive.

Procrastination: Yeah, you're avoiding writing and playing Royal Match or looking up hats for your dog on your phone instead.

Navigating Your Emotions

I think it's important at this early point of the book to emphasize that it's common to experience a wide range of emotions about your writing and editing journey. The act of writing and creating can be hugely emotional!

But it's when you're *only* feeling the negative emotions, experiencing the loss of or lack of joy, and those emotions are having a profound impact or consequences, that you want to start thinking proactively about what changes you may need to make in your mindset, schedule, surroundings, support system and approach.

Below are some tips for navigating these emotions. You're not going to find anything revolutionary or new here, but if this is something you struggle with, hearing these again can be helpful.

If dealing with negative feelings toward your writing has been a particular issue for you, you may even find it helpful to print these out and keep them handy!

Acknowledge Your Feelings: I think this is so important. Too often we tell ourselves that we shouldn't feel something, rather than acknowledging that we do feel it and trying to understand why we're experiencing that emotion. Sometimes, just the act of letting ourselves be in the moment, for a moment, is enough.

Be Aware of Your Emotions: In order to acknowledge something, you need to first be aware of it. Pay attention to what you're feeling, when you're feeling it, even why you're experiencing it. This can help you identify causes, not just symptoms.

Create a Support System: *COMMUNITY MATTERS!* If you've never heard me speak about the importance of community, well, now's your time. Being a writer absolutely can be lonely, difficult and demoralizing. It's crucial to surround yourself with a support system and community that you can depend on to support you in positive, meaningful ways (and no, I'm not talking about toxic positivity, but intentional, real positive support.)

Be Mindful: Do you ever sit at your desk so long that you ignore your body's cues about needing a bathroom break, a stretch break or an eyestrain break? We need to pay attention to those physical cues! Being mindful of your emotional cues is just as crucial. And like physical stretching, more mental techniques such as deep breathing, meditation, or grounding exercises can help regulate emotions.

Express Yourself: Sure, writing is one potential way of expressing yourself, but when it's the writing causing some of the emotions, then you may need other avenues for getting those feelings out. Finding healthy ways to express your emotions, such as video journaling, talking to someone in your support network, physical activity, or engaging in crafts or other hobbies is essential.

Engage in Accessible Physical Activity: Writing is so often sedentary. And in my experience, writers (and other creative types) tend to be over indexed in having some form of neurodiversity, but especially ADHD. Exercise can not only help reduce stress and improve your mood, but it can also help manage some of the symptoms of ADHD and provide a healthy outlet for emotional energy. Getting ourselves moving in whatever way that's accessible is an opportunity to help manage emotions and things like brain fog, mental fatigue and stress.

Set Boundaries: First, boundaries are what you set for yourself, not for other people. That means you're responsible for establishing your boundaries, communicating them clearly, and enforcing them. You must learn to say no (to yourself and to others), abide by your own boundaries, and protect your health and energy. And please remember: you cannot expect others to respect you if you're not first respecting yourself. That means following your own boundaries, not just giving them lip service!

Practice Self-Care: This isn't just about taking time for yourself, giving yourself breaks, and being aware of your own needs (like making sure you're staying hydrated), it's also about being practical with your expectations, being kind to yourself, and choosing to lift yourself up, rather than knock yourself down.

Challenge Negative Thoughts: Negative thoughts are something we all experience, it's a process of going through life. But if your negative thoughts are driving your publishing experience—meaning that's what you're basing your decisions and next steps on—then challenging these thoughts and questioning them, reframing them, and ensuring you're not building your career around them can be crucial. For some people, doing this without assistance of a professional or a support system can be difficult, so please don't think this is something that should be or even can always be done alone.

Seek Professional Help: Therapy is a winning tool and one you shouldn't ignore. Sometimes the root of our overwhelming emotions is something that requires professional guidance. Don't underestimate the importance of treating your mental energy with as much importance and care as you do your physical energy. Look for free resources in your community if paid services aren't an option for you.

Emotions are not linear

One thing to remember about anything that comes with publishing, whether it's writing, editing, marketing, promoting...it's all cyclical. There's no specific end point where you can say you've forever finished a thing.

Because even when you reach the metaphorical End of a book, the next cycle of book creation and publication is waiting right behind it.

That also means that emotions are cyclical as well. You may find that you have high points and low points based on where you're at in your publication cycle, and being aware of that can also help you arm yourself for dealing with those emotions more positively, in a healthy way.

You may also find yourself having or setting unrealistic expectations for yourself and/or your books, and this may play a part in struggling to regulate emotional responses and not throw yourself from one emotional crisis to the next.

When expectations don't meet reality, we may believe we haven't been good enough, haven't done enough, have let others down and have let ourselves down. That means that one of the first, most crucial things we can do to help build our own healthy publishing ecosystem is to create reasonable expectations for ourselves, not set ourselves up for despair with aspirational and unreasonable expectations.

Seek out Joy and Track the Wins

It is so so so easy to get bogged down in everything that's not going right, things that don't feel good, and the negative or difficult aspects of writing, editing and publishing.

That's why it's necessary that we seek out joy and track all of the wins, big and small, as they occur, because we will forget. You'll remember the one negative review, but forget the twenty-five positive, glowing reviews. You'll remember when someone gave you critical feedback on ways to change or improve your manuscript, but you'll forget all the areas they glowingly pointed out that you do well.

This means that you're going to have to make conscious efforts to seek out joy—remind yourself of all the things that you love about writing and publishing. You need to stop and imprint the good moments in your memories, rather than spending all the time ruminating over the negative.

I recommend keeping a folder on your desktop and taking screenshots of positive comments. When you're having a bad day or things are feeling rough, make a conscious point of going into that folder and reading some of those screenshots.

You can also add in a document that you take running notes in of comments people have made to you verbally or somewhere it's difficult to screenshot.

I also find it helpful to print out a few things that are particularly impactful and keep them in my daily note-book or planner. Many years ago, an agent sent me an absolutely beautiful email full of praise and compli-ments, and it was so meaningful and uplifting to me that I printed it out and I transfer it to my new planner every year.

It's also important to track your wins. By this I mean, set an appointment in your calendar every week to review your week, and write down a few things that were wins for you. Stop thinking about the wins as only those big milestones, like release day, but instead think about them as all the smaller milestones you make.

SMALL MILESTONES ADD UP

One way to track and celebrate your small milestones is to ask yourself "What am I proud of doing today, this week, this month?" Those are the moments to remember.

Please believe that these don't have to be huge accomplishments you're tracking, or major milestones. These wins can be moments you're proud of, like sitting down at your computer and writing a sentence, to posting on social media, to being proud of your daily word count. There is no limit to what those wins look like, what's important is that you're acknowledging the progress you're making and the things you're achieving, rather than undervaluing what you do!

One thought I want to leave you with, before we move on to the next chapter: you are a human being, with human emotions, reactions and capabilities.

Treating yourself kindly, setting practical goals, and acknowledging all the things you do well and accomplish is going to help you create a successful publishing ecosystem, and a healthy editing practice, as well as a healthy editing relationship with your critique partners, beta readers, and editors.

TAKE ACTION

How you take action on this chapter is going to vary by individual so I'm offering suggestions below, but the one thing I encourage you to do is commit to taking one action.

1. What area(s) most resonated with you, where you found yourself nodding, or feeling I was talking directly to you?
2. Take action on that section by **creating one small habit or change**. Choose one action that you can implement and test from one of the areas that most spoke to you in this chapter.

Some ideas could be:

- Create a reminder or timer to get up and stretch.
- Set or enforce the boundary of "don't bother your parent/partner/spouse during their writing time."
- Track your water consumption.
- Find a therapist or local support resource.
- Join a healthy writing community (whether online or in person).

3. Commit to tracking your wins, joy and proud moments for one week. Set a daily calendar reminder, choose a way of tracking and place

to track, and pay attention to what you're accomplishing for the next 7 days.

Ask yourself:

- What am I proud of doing today, this week, this month?
- What did I accomplish, complete or make progress on?
- What felt hard but I did it anyway?

Remember, these are things that may seem small but they're not small—you did them! It can be sitting down at your computer and writing a sentence, to posting on social media or answering an email, to showing up for a meeting. Or doing a load of laundry (it doesn't have to be publishing related).

There is no limit to what those wins look like.

CHAPTER 6
AUTHOR VOICE

W hat does your emotional journey through the writing and editing process have to do with author voice, and why am I flowing from that topic to this one?

Everything, it has everything to do with it, because your state of emotions can impact your ability to tap into and access your author voice, as well as connect with your characters and your story. When emotions are troubled, voice can become blocked, whether it's author voice or character voice. And that's how we end up with writer's block.

Don't underestimate the importance of being in tune with your emotional well-being as we enter into these next chapters of editing and writing information.

TL;DR

- Author voice is how you bring a unique personality to the story you're telling.

- Tone, sentence structure, word choices, paragraph length—all of those things add to your voice.
- Character voice is created by you, but is unique to the character.
- Your author voice can change over time, or as a book/story demands.
- The best way to develop your author voice is to write and then write some more!
- When editors and critique partners start to impose absolutes (writing "rules") on your entire body of work, that may be interfering with your voice.
- When someone is helping you polish and make things clear for a good reader experience, that may be a good edit/critique.
- Reader experience is the most important part of creating a story. And story trumps craft.

———

Let me ask you...

Can you define what author voice is?

Can you explain what the aspects of your author voice are?

If you said no to one or both of those questions, you're not alone. Author voice may be one of the most tossed-around but also most misunderstood and hard-to-define phrases in writing.

What is voice?

In genre fiction, voice is what makes an old concept seem fresh and new. It's the quality of storytelling that grabs the reader by the throat and won't let go; it's what defines the reader's relationship to the characters, their perception of the world, and their connection to the story and plot.

An author's voice is what either gives a reader the ability to sink into a story or makes it difficult for them to connect to it.

Author voice is your tone, your flair, the style you bring and the sentence structure you use. It's how you bring a personality to the story, and to the characters.

Throughout the course of my career, I've always placed the idea of author voice at a pinnacle of importance. I've always thought the importance of a writer's voice, as well as character voices, is tremendous, and how you put together sentences and formulate your story is key to how the reader approaches and interacts with your work.

For you as an author, understanding your own voice —whether it's your author voice or your individual characters' voices—can help create a lasting impact on not only your author brand, but also the reader experience and interaction with the story.

Reader experience is an important factor in the writing and editing of a book, and understanding what is/isn't author voice also helps you understand when the reader's experience is more important than how you've written something.

Understanding the difference between what is

and isn't author voice also helps when you're going through edits with another person. When you understand author voice, you gain better insight into when edits are truly stepping on your author voice and when a suggestion or edit is instead something that will improve the reader experience / readability.

How do you define your own author voice?

It can be in the tone, cadence, and rhythm you use. It may be words, slang or other linguistic choices. How you choose to convey the thoughts, emotions and story is all voice.

People may characterize your voice with different things: maybe deadpan humor, snarky protagonists, parenthetical thoughts, stream of consciousness writing, or creative word choice.

There is *no one thing* that creates author voice, but instead it's how you, the storyteller, engage the reader with the story and give them the narrative voice and characters' voices on page through a variety of ways, to deliver the best reading experience.

Put another way, your author voice is how you take the elements of writing a story and bring them together in your unique way. Alongside this, your author voice is also which elements of writing and storytelling are stronger (and strongest) when the story is written by you.

When you're trying to understand author voice, think about reading this book, written in my voice. You can start to pick out some elements of my voice the more you read.

For instance, I write somewhat informally but with enough formality to suggest confidence in my topic. I show snippets of humor here and there, as the topic allows, and I am a fan of parenthetical thoughts. I would say that my voice also conveys a sense of empathy toward authors who are trying to learn, and I break concepts down into digestible, but understandable pieces in order to help authors absorb the content.

All of those things create *my* author voice.

But, Angela, what about when we're reading and writing fiction?

Here are a few present-day fiction authors with strong or recognizable author voices: Kennedy Ryan, Martha Wells, Sonali Dev, N.K. Jemisin, May Peterson, Kristen Ashley, T. Kingfisher, Benjamin Stevenson, Anna Lee Huber, Stephen King.

I can't excerpt their works here as examples due to copyright, but take some time to view some samples and think about the individual voices of these authors.

Because I do think examples are an important part of learning about author voice, I asked a variety of authors to help me out with an exercise.

For this exercise, I gave the authors the following prompt and asked them to either write up to 250 words based on this prompt or pull a passage that fit from an existing book they'd written in the past:

There were no instructions, other than the one-sentence prompt, and I didn't tell any of the authors what the snippet was for, other than use in this book.

As you read the snippets, you'll notice that each

author used different word choices, sentence structure, dialogue, point of view, tense, descriptors...each one is unique and gives you insight into their individual voice, genre and style choices.

And that's what your author voice is—your choices.

The prompt: *Your POV character notices another character looking at them*

 I look up to find all the men staring at me again. The Elder is leaning heavily on his cane, but there's still a quiet strength in the way he holds himself. He's studying me like I'm a puzzle with half the pieces missing. Like he's uncertain of the full picture, but he recognizes the shape all the same. Lyathin's gaze lingers in a way that makes me want to hold Ryot's hand and not let go. He's staring at me with something deeper than distrust. I think I've ruined his carefully ordered world just by existing.

And Ryot...his eyes stay on me for a second too long, like he wants to look away but can't.

"Get her to the infirmary," Archon Lyathin barks.

Ryot drops my hand.

I feel the loss immediately, but that's because his warmth was starting to ease the pain. I don't let myself consider it's anything else.

 He was watching her with a small, mysterious smile playing over his lips and he would've captured her with his gaze if she'd allowed eye contact. She was sure of it. The same intuition that had her excited about this man warned her to proceed with at least a little bit of caution.

It was like the desire to be near a wild animal, knowing it had the capacity to hurt her, but also knowing that if she remained calm and didn't provoke it, she would have the experience of a lifetime.

"Why?" She finally lifted her gaze to meet his. Why had he said anything at all?

Damn, he was a captivating man. He was immaculately dressed in a European-cut suit, sleek and fitted to his lanky frame that hinted at a fit physique. He exuded sophistication with an aristocratic air, and that alone would have—should have—turned heads. But no one else seemed to have noticed him, nor was he paying attention to anyone else but her. And that was exciting, too.

"You are in danger." He made the statement a simple fact. All seriousness, no wry humor.

She tilted her head. It was a line in any number of plays, movies, television shows, and probably in countless books. But his expression was completely neutral, and that unsettled her. Wouldn't someone trying to convince her of any kind of threat to her safety have at least a little bit of urgency in their tone? Wouldn't they at least sound like they cared if she believed them?

She raised an eyebrow. "Everyone in the theater, or just me?"

She thought the corner of his mouth quirked farther upward for a split second. "At the moment, just you."

Excerpt from *Wings Once Cursed and Bound* by Piper J. Drake, ©2023 by Lalana Dararutana. Used by permission of Sourcebooks, LLC. All rights reserved.

 Three eyes stared at Wouter when he came to, set into an adorably tiny and decidedly non-bani face. Two large round ones and a tiny one above them in the middle. They blinked as they stared right back. Its growl seemed similar to what he'd heard before he passed out. Deep and dark for such a tiny creature. It was cute, though. Cute as a tiny, short-legged deer with leaves on its head instead of antlers. "Hey, little buddy."

It tilted its head and raised a paw, squishing something against Wouter's lips. It burst open, spreading meaty residue across his mouth with a sour bite to it. He licked his lips clean—getting an aftertaste of sunscreen along with it—and found another one smooshed against his tongue.

After Wouter cleaned the remaining residue off his lips, the creature tilted its head the other way as if it was studying him.

"Thank you." He hoped they weren't poisonous. Not when his stomach seemed to have settled after throwing up. That plant in the cave must have been dangerous. "I hope that was you growling, and not your parents. I don't think I'm fit enough to fight them."

Excerpt from *How Six Saved the Frogs* by Blaine D. Arden, ©2024. Used by permission of Blaine D. Arden. All Rights Reserved.

"I *want* to tell you. Especially since we both like comics." She winked again and this time there was no mistaking her flirtation.

Phượng took a swig of her drink to avoid responding and possibly fucking up her chances of getting to know the woman who literally dropped into her life.

"My sweet—but not too sweet—and sexy feeling was *you*."

Phượng choked, spitting her drink all over Hoàng. So much for keeping her cool. She grabbed a handful of thin cocktail napkins from behind the bar.

"I'm so sorry." If only she were a shapeshifter instead of a potions master so she could make herself disappear into thin air.

"It's only—" Hoàng sniffed, "—gin?"

She grabbed Phượng's wrists as she attempted to dab the liquor off Hoàng's shirt. Phượng froze.

"But you already knew that my thoughts weren't warm. They were smoking hot." Hoàng locked eyes with Phượng in unmistakable desire.

Phượng's chest tightened and she struggled to breathe. Hoàng's energy that she invoked earlier flooded through Phượng. Her entire body flashed with a heat so hot it could be mistaken for a chill. Her fingers clenched around the napkin as she stared at blue-haired woman's soft lips.

Those lips turned into a grin that promised much more than a kiss. Phượng looked away.

"I'm not good with people," Phượng confessed as she ignored the heat in her cheeks. "That's why I sit here at every happy hour and hope that an extrovert will adopt me. I don't want to be anti-social. It's just hard."

Great, now she was rambling. She wished she was in her lab working on potions instead of talking to other humans.

Hoàng squeezed Phượng's hands.

"I'd love to be your extrovert."

Excerpt from *The Taste of Memories* by Thien-Kim Lam, ©2025. Used by permission of Thien-Kim Lam. All Rights Reserved.

What was left of the moon was bright, but the winter sky was coal. Timothy's eyes darted from one side of the road to the other. He could almost make out the stucco houses on each side, but the street ahead of him was black. The ocean roared behind the house on his left. He squinted, looking behind it. Lines of foam jumped in the air, but the waves they were attached to disappeared in the dark. He took a deep breath. Ocean air. Nothing like it.

Suddenly, he tensed. Timothy turned fast. Left. Right. Front of the street. Behind him. There was no one else in the street. Was there?

He pulled up the sleeve on his hoodie, and increased his pace. His watch glared in the night. 9:06 PM. None of the houses had lights on. Too early for bed. Wasn't it? Was he the only person in this neighborhood? Things you never thought to ask Airbnb.

Feet. Running. He turned.

Left. Right. Front. Back. Still, no one.

Timothy pulled his hood up. His hand glazed the back of his neck. The hair was standing straight up. His father's voice echoed. *Stand your ground.*

He turned. The yard to his left. Was someone in the car in the driveway? Behind it?

Running again. Other side of the street.

Timothy turned.

He laughed, and took a deep breath as the fox ran by, a rabbit, in front of it. Poor rabbit.

Timothy turned back, and saw the man.

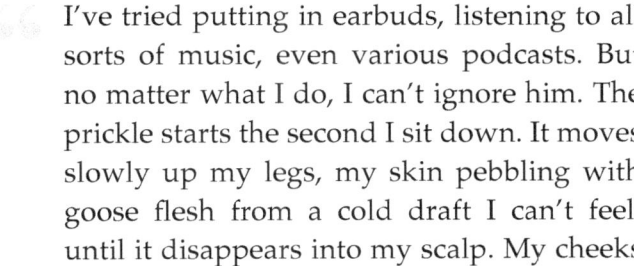 I've tried putting in earbuds, listening to all sorts of music, even various podcasts. But no matter what I do, I can't ignore him. The prickle starts the second I sit down. It moves slowly up my legs, my skin pebbling with goose flesh from a cold draft I can't feel, until it disappears into my scalp. My cheeks flood with color as the blood rushes to the surface before blotching its way across my neck. He's staring.

And if I look up, I'll get caught in those black eyes, again, unable to look away as my heart hammers in my chest.

Maybe I shouldn't come back here. I frown. This totally sucks. Tomorrow's my last free day before I have to see Joel at dinner. Ugh. Twenty-four hours left for me to figure out how to break up with him. I've been loving my evenings free of his moody discussions, way too much. I don't want to tiptoe around him anymore. Somehow, I have to end our engagement. A small headache brews at my temples, and I rub them, closing my eyes. If I'm not going to enjoy my time here, I should just leave.

"What the fuck's wrong with *you*?"

The voice hasn't changed from the last time the man spoke to me. Clipped. Emotionless. My frown deepens before I raise my eyes to meet his dark ones. Great. This is just what I need. I force my lips to lift in a smile.

She never notices me, but that's okay. I notice her all the time. The little things. How she bites her fingernails when she's deep in thought or nervous. How she places her other hand at the nape of her neck for support. How her eyes light up when she's excited. I don't want to disturb her; I don't want to creep her out because I'm honestly not that kind of guy. I'm just...shy.

"Martin... Just go over there and talk to her. A week is long enough." My best friend Chase scoffs, smirking.

Rolling my eyes, I glance up in her direction, and she softly smiles at me.

Maybe that's my in...? Maybe I can go over there now and stop being so shy?

Once she waves at me, I'm out of my seat on autopilot. My heart pounds with every step I take. I don't even know how this conversation will go, but here's my chance. I stand in front of her, placing my hands behind my back, offering her a smile.

"I was wondering if you were going to come over and say something. I'm Shelby."

I watch a blush spread across her cheeks, and it warms me, too.

"I'm Martin."

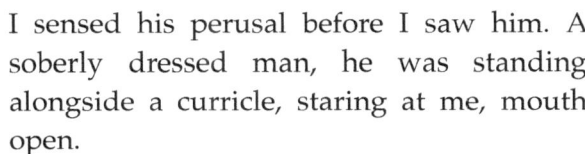

I sensed his perusal before I saw him. A soberly dressed man, he was standing alongside a curricle, staring at me, mouth open.

"Hello," I smiled, walking towards him. "I'm Mary Sheriff. Are you here to take me to Clifton Hall?"

"Oh…beg pardon," he stuttered, his face now shiny and pink. "That's to say. Welcome, Miss Sheriff. Ronald Mainwaring. That's me—my name."

His voice cracked and he squeezed shut his eyes. Poor man, perhaps he wasn't used to people?

When he reopened them, his voice was firmer, "might I help you into the curricle?"

When I took his hand, I was surprised by how warm and firm it was. He helped me settle into place, then grabbed my portmanteau as though it weighed nothing, placing it by my feet.

"Yours?" he pointed at Papa's battered old leather trunk.

I nodded. The familiar wave of grief

engulfed me and I was barely aware of the trunk being strapped on and the man jumping up beside me and flicking the reins.

The clip-clopping of the horses and the gentle swaying motion gradually soothed my sadness and I looked about me. It was a glorious September day, the leaves beginning to turn golden, and everywhere was bathed in the late afternoon sunshine.

"How beautiful it is!" I grinned at him.

"Beautiful indeed," he responded, but he was looking straight at me, an intense glow in his blue eyes.

Angie stood not ten feet away. His blood heated. She did that to him. And his cock took notice too.

She lowered those lush lashes before her gaze skimmed down his body to stop at his groin.

When their gazes reconnected, he saw the need and raw desire there. Now was the time to deal with Angie and find out what she really wanted.

Her eyes widened as his body pressed

against hers. "Yes, or no?" he hoarsely rasped. When she didn't answer. "I'm done playing games."

She trembled slightly against him and he was about to back off when she licked her lips and said, "Yes. Oh yes."

Consent. He leaned down and took her lips with his, thrusting his tongue into her mouth. He tasted the slight sweetness from what he thought was the wedding cake, but probably was Angie's own natural taste. He broke the kiss, and she leaned on him as if she couldn't stand on her own two legs.

Elation filled him. She wasn't running or telling him off. "I'm not like other men." Would she be able to handle his compelling need for dominance?

"I don't want other men. I want you."

"Fine. I understand you have the next two weeks off. You can spend them here, but if you stay, you'll play by my rules. I'll be the one in charge. The rest we can discuss later."

Excerpt from *Tangled Temptation* by Marie Tuhart, ©2025. Used by permission of Marie Tuhart. All Rights Reserved.

How do I recognize what my voice is?

When you start getting repeat comments from critique partners, editors, beta readers and readers/reviews that note specific things, you may start to realize that's part of your voice.

You may also naturally have a strong voice that feels recognizable and instantly seen on page.

Recognizing your own voice can be difficult at first, especially as you're getting started writing and crafting stories. Your voice may develop over time, and you can deliberately choose to lean into certain aspects of your voice, while also choosing to work to eliminate other aspects of your voice.

One way to begin to determine what your own author voice is, is to be conscious of your own choices, and to take time to analyze those choices and ask questions of yourself about those choices.

Questions you can ask to start determining voice, whether it's in your own work or someone else's

What themes am I drawn to?

Reflect on the recurring themes in your work. This can help identify what drives your storytelling and what matters most in your narratives.

How do the readers feel after reading?

Consider the emotions evoked in your readers. This could range from joy, suspense, comfort, to curiosity. Which emotions are most effectively conveyed? Are there any emotions that are strongly evoked book over book?

What distinguishes my/their writing style?

Analyze the stylistic elements that make your writing unique—be it your sentence structure, use of dialogue, descriptive detail, or lyrical quality. Do you notice any patterns? Is there something that you favor and seem to use or fall back on?

Who are my/their writing influences?

Can you see anything of writers you may be emulating or have been influenced by? Understanding this may help you further pinpoint how your personal style is reflected in your books.

What do the reviews say about my/their voice? What do editors, critique partners or beta readers note about my voice?

External perspective is an excellent source of insight into your own voice and style. It can give you hints (or outright tell you) how others perceive your voice and help you gain more clarity.

How is my character different from other characters (and from me, the author?)

Characterization, by definition, is the idea of creating a character who is distinctive, has unique features— whether personality, appearance, mannerisms, quirks, emotions or otherwise—or something about their nature that isn't like that of others. Understanding what makes your character(s) unique is going to help you develop their unique and authentic character voice that's both different from yours and from your other characters' voices.

How does my character's voice differ from my narrative voice?

Assess how you adapt your voice to different characters or narratives. This can highlight your flexibility and the range of your voice, but can also highlight if you don't have enough flexibility and range in your voice, and all of your characters have a similar voice. Voice works the same whether you're writing fiction or non-fiction, but fiction becomes even more complicated in terms of voice, because we also add in the layers of character voices, not just one author voice.

How do I develop my author voice?

Write. Write often. Developing your author voice and getting to know how you write and how you put together the story and the characters and the world all comes down to practice. Often, authors won't discover their author voice until they've written several books, because they're working on the quality of writing and storytelling. So to discover your author voice, you have to write, try new things, explore craft, understand structure (sentence and story) and get a feel for what feels most natural to you as you're writing.

Can your voice change?

Yes. I think especially for newer authors, as they're exploring their writing style and growing into their craft, voice isn't always apparent. It can take time to develop a consistent writing style, as well as writing craft. Sometimes when craft starts out awkward or new, voice isn't apparent at all, because the new writer is focused on the mechanics of writing and storytelling. So voice can take time to develop and nurture.

It can also change or be different based on genre or story. Some authors have such a strong voice that it carries through everything they do, while others may have the ability to switch their voice based on their genre.

What is character voice?

Character voice is when an author creates for each character their own distinct narrative, pattern of speaking, favorite words and phrases, word choices, phrasing, accent, and sentence structure.

One of the most difficult things to do naturally, and can be a higher-level writing skill to learn, is creating these distinct character voices in both narrative and dialogue, for main characters and secondary characters.

Sometimes, an author has such a strong internal voice of their own that comes through in their writing, that it can be a struggle to make the characters sound distinct from one another in a way that makes it obvious to a reader which character is speaking or which character's narrative they're reading.

It can be as simple as word choices. A few times during edits, I've given an author an editorial note that says "This character wouldn't use this word. This is author intrusion. Or this is a word/phrase the other main character would use."

What is author intrusion?

Author intrusion, simply put, is when the author doesn't consider the character they've created and developed as separate from the author, and instead of writing choices, actions, thoughts, feelings, dialogue, phrasing, and words that feel natural to the character they've developed, the author temporarily inserts themselves and their choices into the story in place of the character.

This creates a scenario that can cause a disconnect for the reader, throw them out of the story, confuse them or make them feel as if the character has been written inconsistently.

How do I develop character voice?

Part of creating characterization is also creating character voice. Here are some choices you can make for your character (or your character can make for themselves, if you're a writer whose characters seem to speak to you organically):

- **Language:** What is their primary language?
- **Accent/dialect**: Do they have a distinct accent or dialect?

- **Word choices:** Are there words they use frequently?
- **Phrasing:** Do they have favorite phrases?
- **What's their sentence structure like?** For instance, in motorcycle club romances, it's popular to have the male main character speak in clipped sentences, often leaving off a subject from the beginning.
- **What type of internal dialogue* do they have with themselves?** Does your character speak to themselves as if they're an outside observer? Do they have full sentences of internal dialogue? Do they use expletives in internal dialogue? Maybe they make astute observations in internal dialogue?
- **In terms of narrative, what do they observe?** For example, in JD Robb's *...in Death* series, the main character, Eve Dallas, is noted as a person who observes the details of the room and the people in it almost subconsciously.
- **Also in narrative*, do they express what they're feeling, thinking?**
- **Do they have a certain tone they use often?** Sarcasm, humor, anger, irritability, empathy, kindness.
- **How do they speak?** Are they abrupt, patient, soft-spoken, loud, etc?

Internal dialogue and narrative are two different things:

- **Internal dialogue** *is an interior conversation the point of view character has with themselves. No one else is involved in this "dialogue" but it's instead the act of speaking directly to themselves. Sometimes the line between internal dialogue and deep narrative is thin.*
- **Narrative** *is simply things that aren't dialogue (with another person or out loud) that tell the reader the story. Narrative can be shallow or deep, but even deep narrative isn't internal dialogue.*

When are edits *not* interfering with my voice?

By definition, editing is meant to give you a different outlook on the story, elements, and characters, and is meant to make and suggest changes. So I always encourage authors to remember that not agreeing with a suggestion or edit doesn't mean the editor has interfered with your voice. It can simply be a difference of opinion or difference of vision for the story, and that is an absolutely natural part of editing.

Here are things that I would generally not consider as interfering with author voice. (I say in general because there are always going to be exceptions).

- Correcting punctuation
- Suggesting small changes to word choice, phrasing and sentence structure.
- Anything that makes the reading flow more smoothly/improves reading comprehension (for example, rearranging sentences)

- Pointing out repetition (of words, phrasing and sentence structure)
- Marking problematic passages or language
- Edits that enhance or improve the reader's experience by furthering their understanding or clarifying. Everything above is included in that list, but there may be other scenarios in which an edit is meant to improve the reading experience. This is why it's important to evaluate edits on an edit by edit basis, not just refuse something because you hate the Oxford comma, for instance. Sometimes the Oxford comma truly is necessary for clarity.

And I want to emphasize again that suggesting big story changes, giving characterization critique, offering plot suggestions, and asking for revisions and even major deletions of scenes or changes to the beginning/end are absolutely the things that you can expect to see for developmental edits. (And want to see! Remember, making these types of story/character changes is where the editing magic happens, *not* in changing punctuation.)

During the course of having beta readers review this book, one of my authors doing a beta read left this comment and I decided to include her additional advice —in her voice:

 You might include deleting entire character POV's or entire characters (both of which you recommended to me in different projects, both of which made for a better reader experience). Yes,

> *it hurts to get that type of advice, but it hurts*
> *less to know it will enhance the overall reader*
> *experience which is the goal of content editing.*

One final thought: I always (always) expect my authors to disagree with me on some edits. But not agreeing with changes or even an editor and author not having the same vision for the story is *not* voice interference, it's just a natural difference of subjective opinion.

If you're struggling with the concept of large editorial changes not being an interference with your voice, it may be a good opportunity to reflect on whether you're actually open to feedback and want to be edited. And it is a choice/option not to have someone else edit/critique your work, but it takes being honest with yourself and making that choice, rather than deciding others are always giving invalid feedback.

When are edits interfering with my voice?

When edits/suggestions may interfere is in cases where the author feels as if the editor or critique partner doesn't have a good reason for the changes other than "it sounds better to them" or if the suggestion so fundamentally changes how you tell the story that you wouldn't even recognize it as yours any longer.

The one thing that is so important in the editorial and critique process, no matter who you're seeking feedback from, is making sure that you've attempted to clearly explain your vision for the story. I have worked with many authors, and it's always the *most* difficult when all I have is a manuscript with no idea of what the author is trying to achieve with the story.

For examples of when edits may be interfering with your voice, I am so fortunate to be able to use examples that authors have shared with me over the years. I've bolded a key sentence in each that gives you a clue as to why it's the difference between a critique that improves the story and a critique that clashes with the author's vision for the work.

> *I once had a critique partner in a workshop tell me I should make my piece funny "like Bridget Jones style." I was totally taken aback. **I'm not funny. Basically, she was saying she didn't like it as it was. (Which is fine. I like to write drama.)***
>
> *The workshop leader spoke after her and said I should continue doing what I do. He spoke with me after the meeting too to make sure I understood that what I was doing was fine and didn't require comedy.*

> *A comment I got from a critique partner (first time we were exchanging work) they recommended I write the story over switching everything from first person to third person. **They didn't provide clear reasoning for the choice other than their preference was to read stories in third person.** My book was a contemporary romance. If I'd been writing historical, or even fantasy romance, I may have understood the suggestion. But the moment I*

read that comment, I knew we just wouldn't mesh moving forward.

> My agent HATED BookX. **She said the way they talked was not realistic and no one actually lived that way in rural America.**
>
> I asked to put her on hold so I could call my cousin.
>
> BookX still gets "THANK YOU for writing a book about where I'm from" emails from all over non-urban/suburban America and I'm glad I stuck to it.

————

In 2021, when I first wrote about author voice for a lesson in *Before You Hit Send®*, a tweet crossed my timeline from Geraint Evans that so vividly illustrates voice versus editing out voice, that I had to share it.

The author of the tweet was specifically speaking about writing with ADHD, but this type of example is excellent for showing the change in manuscript voice after having gone through an overly restrictive and voice-killing editing session.

This tweet shows two examples side by side, with the heading: How ADHD people write VS how we have to write. I've included an image of the original tweet, along with the two images that were in the tweet, and the text of each image below it.

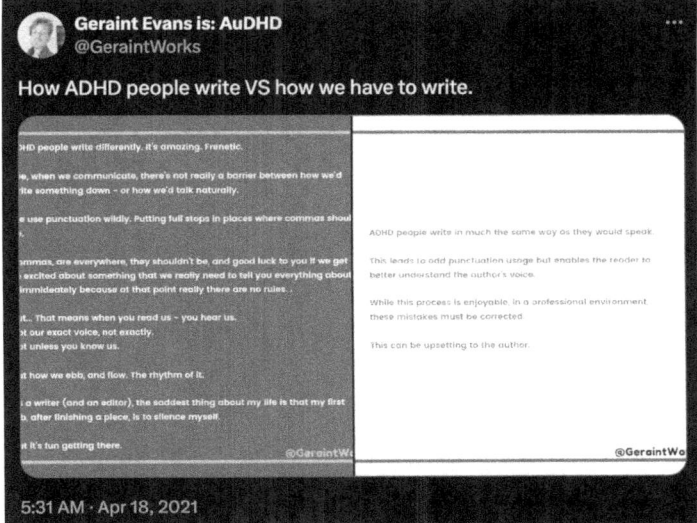

Image 1 Text:

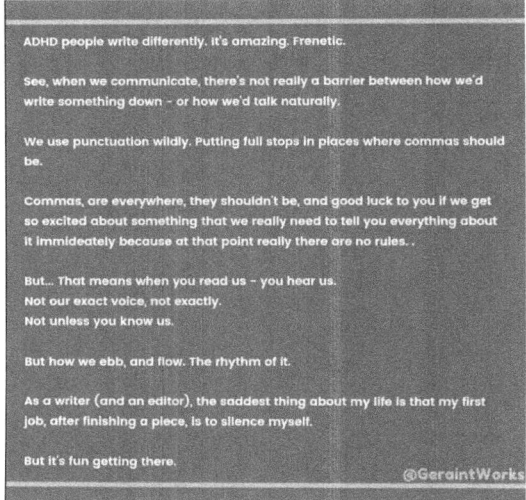

ADHD people write differently. It's amazing. Frenetic.

See, when we communicate, there's not really a barrier between how we'd write something down - or how we'd talk naturally.

We use punctuation wildly. Putting full stops in places where commas should be.

Commas, are everywhere, they shouldn't be, and good luck to you if we get so excited about something that we really need to tell you everything about it immideately because at that point really there are no rules. .

But... That means when you read us - you hear us.
Not our exact voice, not exactly.
Not unless you know us.

But how we ebb, and flow. The rhythm of it.

As a writer (and an editor), the saddest thing about my life is that my first job, after finishing a piece, is to silence myself.

But it's fun getting there.

@GeraintWorks

ADHD people write differently. It's amazing. Frenetic.

See, when we communicate, there's not really a barrier between how we'd write something down - or how we'd talk naturally.

We use punctuation wildly. Putting full stops in places where commas should be.

Commas, are everywhere, they shouldn't be, and good luck to you if we got so excited about something that we really need to tell you everything about it immideately because at that point there really are no rules.

But... That means when you read us - you hear us.

Not our exact voice, not exactly.

Not unless you know us.

But how we ebb, and flow. The rhythm of it.

As a writer (and an editor), the saddest thing about my life is that my first job, after finishing a piece, is to silence myself.

But it's fun getting there.

Image 2:

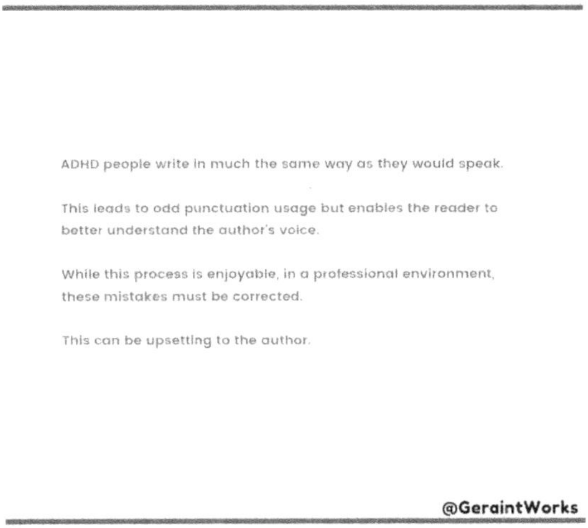

ADHD people write in much the same way as they would speak.

This leads to odd punctuation usage but enables the reader to better understand the author's voice.

While this process is enjoyable, in a professional environment, these mistakes must be corrected.

This can be upsetting to the author.

@GeraintWorks

Image 2 text:

> ADHD people write in much the same way as they would speak.
>
> This leads to odd punctuation usage but enables the reader to better understand the author's voice.
>
> While this process is enjoyable, in a professional environment, these mistakes must be corrected.
>
> This can be upsetting to the author.

This post struck a chord with me, perhaps not incidentally because I also have ADHD and I spend a lot of time, including during the writing and editing of this book, trying to pull back at least somewhat on my stream of consciousness, twisty, long sentences, and overuse of certain words.

This example also highlights why AI can't quite capture unique voice, or replicate your cadence, and why it's not a substitute for writing your story yourself —because AI will always fall back on making things clear, following the "rules" it's learned, and imitating what it's been fed, without being able to conceptualize on its own.

It's also for this reason that sometimes I deliberately feed what I've written into AI, and ask it to "clean it up" when I need it to be as clear as possible. For example, I do this with instructions (like the instructions for beta reading this book) and long emails with a lot of information that I need to put in logical bullet points so the reader doesn't miss any information. AI will take my chatty voice and make it make a little more logical sense for the times when it needs to make logical sense. But it doesn't sound like me.

So in the case where I deliberately ask AI to help me clean up an email or instructions I've written , is AI interfering with my voice? No, since I'm *asking* it to do this, knowing AI will re-arrange and rewrite.

But what if I didn't request that, and someone went in and completely rewrote my words to sound different?

This is where it can be tough to figure out the line between editing and interfering with an author's voice.

If I asked someone to edit my work, and they rewrote a sentence, I might initially feel it was interfering with my voice **but** if it provides clarity when it's needed, and the *clarity is more important than the way I've* *phrased it*, then the answer is probably no, it's not interfering with my author voice, it's giving a necessary change to *improve the reader experience* (and in this case, reader experience is more important than how I originally wrote the sentence).

However, if the change removes my voice, and *the way it's said was more important than total clarity*, then yes, I might feel the person making the change is interfering with my voice because in this case, the reader's best experience comes from experiencing *my* voice.

As you can tell in this section, there isn't a checklist I can provide or an objective "yes or no" list to be had about what is interfering with your voice and what isn't. Instead, *this is a good reminder that editing does require us to set our ego aside and ask ourselves what's best for the book and for the reader experience.*

The idea of whether something is interfering with your voice, or providing a better reader experience, is a subjective thing that needs to be taken on a case-by-case basis. The most important thing is that you not automatically assign all changes and revisions as being "bad" or "good" but evaluate them each on their own merit, and be willing to have a discussion with your editor, critique partner or beta reader while being open to the idea that there will always be some changes suggested that really are better than the way you originally wrote it.

Your Voice, Your Story, Your Readers

I'm going to repeat a paragraph I wrote at the beginning of this chapter:

Throughout the course of my career, I've always placed the idea of author voice at a pinnacle of importance. I've always thought the importance of a writer's voice, as well as character voices, is tremendous, and how you put together sentences and formulate your story is key to how the reader approaches and interacts with your work.

However, over the past decade, it's also become apparent to me that there are times when editors, especially in traditional publishing, have attempted to homogenize voices and, more specifically, whitewash voices by trying to force authors to adhere to certain "standards" of English or language use.

It's in cases like these where we see Black, Indigenous, and other authors of color in particular have their natural author voices interfered with and disrespected. And it's important to remember that this is not what editing and critique is meant to do.

Sidenote: Because I'm white, I say it's become apparent to me over the past decade as I've increased my learning and listening, but this has certainly not only been a new issue that just started in the past decade. This is a historic problem authors of historically marginalized backgrounds have faced and continue to experience.

Here's a specific, painful example of this that was shared with me (and is used with permission):

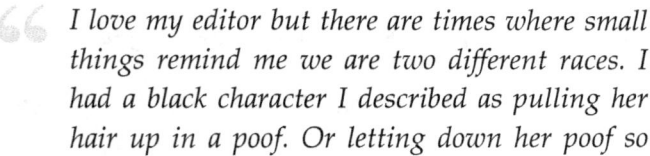

> *I love my editor but there are times where small things remind me we are two different races. I had a black character I described as pulling her hair up in a poof. Or letting down her poof so*

her curls could hang about her shoulders. My character was black and had natural hair. The editor commented each time that she couldn't imagine what this hairstyle was and that she was imagining someone who looked like a poodle and I should be more clear. I don't think she meant it cruelly but it was the oblivious nature that stung a bit. I felt like she glossed over my character's identity as a black woman so it didn't stick with her.

As we move into greater awareness of cultural, racial, ethnic, gender, sex, and other differences in writing, it's important that we understand how our default biases can impact how we interact with writing as editors, critique partners, and even readers.

Stop using the phrase "proper English"

There is no such thing as "proper" English, for you or your characters. There is only what's best for your book.

I think this is an especially important point for editors to remember as we welcome more voices and become more inclusive as a publishing community. All voices are not the same, and should not use the same phrasing, wording, syntax, or grammar choices. To artificially enforce an idea of "good" or "right" or "proper" across voices is to try to homogenize instead of celebrating an author's unique voice.

As I've followed a number of linguists via social media, I've learned a lot about unpacking the privilege of language, and that translates to author voice as well.

Linguist Rob Drummond gave me permission to quote him so I'm sharing these points Rob wrote about language, because they're important to remember as you both write and edit, whether editing for yourself or someone else.

In particular, please pay attention to 1 and 2, and 8 and 9:

1. Standard English is no better than other varieties, it just has a history of powerful people behind it.
2. Most grammar "rules" that people get upset about aren't actually rules at all.
3. Texting/messaging isn't ruining the language.
4. Language is perfectly safe in the hands of young people.
5. Of course we need to teach young people to use standard English. But we can do so without belittling any other varieties they use.
6. Words can change meaning through usage.
7. All of the above does not mean "anything goes"; language is about contextual appropriateness, not arbitrary notions of "correctness".
8. Criticizing people's language is always about more than language.
9. It's natural to have linguistic preferences; it's only a problem when those preferences

become a tool with which to negatively judge other people.

YOUR AUTHOR VOICE

All of linguist Rob Drummond's points add up to the idea that we must let go of the assertion that there's one "correct" way of storytelling or a "right" way for an author's voice to be portrayed.

It's also useful to remember that all of those "rules" of grammar and writing and "standards of English" that you learned in school often don't need to be strictly applied outside of an academic setting.

How you once wrote a paper based on each teacher or professor's guidelines and preferred style isn't necessarily how you should think of writing your book, whether it's a novel or a non-fiction book about editing.

I'll say this more than once in this book and I'm saying it again here: your readers aren't going to fall in love with your book based on an excellent use of punctuation or ability to cite sources.

So as you read this book, what I hope you take away isn't a sense of restriction because it seems as if I'm sharing a bunch of writing "rules". But instead, I want you to take away a sense of freedom in knowing what the elements of grammar and craft look like, so you as a writer, and/or editor, can use those elements to greatest advantage for each unique, individual work in order to provide the best reading experience.

Remember: your voice is what draws readers to your work, and back again. The elements of craft are what hold the story and the reading experience together in a way that's most pleasing and compelling and keep them happy to spend their time and money on the story.

TAKE ACTION

This requires you to ask yourself some questions to start the process of thinking about and identifying components of your author voice.

Hot tip! Knowing components of your author voice is a strong foundation for understanding your author brand and leaning in to marketing to the right audience.

Ask yourself:

- Is there something in your writing that you can already recognize as part of your developing author voice or that is found consistently in your backlist?
- Can you think of a time working with an editor, beta reader, or critique partner when you felt they really respected your voice?
- Perhaps there's a time you felt someone didn't understand or was interfering with

your author or character voice? What was it that they did or suggested you change that felt as if your voice was being stripped?

- Do you have published books? Look at the reviews and see what themes are common when people talk about your writing and story telling.
- One of my beta readers said she looks at what Goodreads shelves readers had put her book on, and it provided her with a list of themes and tropes and keywords to start with.
- Ask your readers what they like about your writing.
- If you're not published or working on your first book, ask yourself some of the questions I posed earlier in this chapter, in the section titled "How do I recognize what my voice is?" These are questions you can ask, to start determining voice, whether it's in your own work or someone else's.

TIPS & TIDBITS

Author Question: What to do when you get conflicting advice on voice. You have no voice, to this is not the right voice, to this voice is amazing.

Angela's Response: This is such a good question. I looked for a place to work this into the text, but I don't want it to get lost among everything else so I'm leaving it here.

You are going to get conflicting advice. Full stop. Whether it's from different editors, different critique partners or different beta readers.

You'll see this in action in book reviews. Choose a favorite book that you love. Think about the things you love about that book, why it makes you happy, why you recommend it. Now go look at the reviews on that book. In particular, look at the 1- and 2-star reviews. Did they love and appreciate the same things you did? Likely not.

We know reading is subjective, and editing is equally subjective.

What's an author to do? (I know, that was the original question.)

1. First, this is why it's incredibly important to know your author brand, to understand your own author voice, and begin to be aware of what elements of your voice are part of your brand and your readers' expectations. If you don't know what your brand and voice are, you will change things in response to every comment you get.

2. Equally important to know your goals for your story, what story you want to tell, and the experience you want the readers to have with the story.

3. Be discerning about who you work with. Not everyone is qualified to give you feedback, and you shouldn't listen to everyone who gives it. Don't crowdsource 50 opinions on your book, but instead find people who have

experience—especially those with more experience than you—and who you resonate with when you hear their advice.

4. Have confidence in yourself. Yeah, this isn't therapy but that does mean some of you need to learn to love your writing, love your stories, love your characters and believe in the choices you're making. Having confidence does come with practice and experience, so that means… keep writing. The next book and the next!

5. Give the advice you do get due consideration, and when it's conflicting, decide whose opinion you're weighting heavier. You don't need to be listening to anyone 100% of the time but there should be people on your team you trust to have the best interests of you, your story and your readers as a high priority.

CHAPTER 7
EFF THE WRITING "RULES"

I know having "rules" and absolutes to follow can be comforting. Having someone tell you exactly what not to do is almost as great as someone telling you exactly what to do.

But writing "rules" are not a magic solution to winning readers and creating fans.

This is an important lesson because I *super-duper* want you to know and remember three things:

1. My philosophy on writing "rules" is that there are no rules. In fact, the title of this chapter should tell you what I think about writing "rules"! I hope you'll embrace this philosophy while also embracing a great reading experience for readers.
2. I'm not a grammar purist (and you shouldn't be either).
3. We will especially not use the words "proper English" or "standard English" when talking

about writing. (see previous chapter for more on this).

Why do I *super-duper* want you to know this?

Because I have seen far too many authors and editors (and critique partners and beta readers…) get bound up in the idea of writing "rules" to the exclusion of actually embracing their natural storytelling ability and perhaps diluting their author voice or character voices. And get so bound up in the idea of writing "rules" that they only focus on editing for these "rules" and not actually editing for things that will enhance the story and the reader's experience.

TL;DR

- When editors and critique partners start to impose absolutes (writing "rules") on your entire body of work, that may be interfering with your voice.
- Reader experience is the most important part of creating a story. And story trumps craft.
- There are no "rules".

_____

Zero. None.

Most "rules" come with good intentions, to help writers improve craft, to possibly make a book more readable, to give readers the best reader experience.

But ultimately, what happens when we focus too much on "rules" is that writers tend to hyper focus on these subjective writing guidelines in a way that's either not materially changing what's important—story, characters, pacing, world-building, etc.—or in a way that changes their natural author voice to its detriment, making it lose some of its sparkle, become more uniform or robotic, and taking out the parts that make the voice (author and/or character) stand out and feel distinct.

Having "rules" and absolutes to follow can be comforting. I started the chapter with that line because it's something that's true for all of us. Whether we're writing, editing, indie-publishing our first book, feeding sourdough starter, exercising, learning guitar—whatever it is, having an exact process to follow conserves energy, makes it feel less daunting, and encourages us to keep moving forward because it just feels easier.

When we think about writing "rules", they're often rules about what not to do, and having someone tell you exactly what not to do is almost as great as someone telling you exactly what to do. Because it still creates a roadmap to follow, and having a roadmap is often much easier than just conjuring up something wholesale yourself.

And so, at some point as you hire me as your editor, take my editing course, attend my workshops, or read my books on editing, you're going to say, "Angela, how many exclamation points is too many?" and "Exactly how long should my chapters be?" And I may be forced to give you guidelines (because guidelines do help) but

I want to make it clear: *they're not rules and it's okay to do something entirely different.*

What do you mean by "rules", anyway?

If you're just starting out on your writing and editing journey, you may be a bit confused by what I mean by writing rules.

If you've been doing this a while, I'll bet you could write a whole list for me.

Writing rules are the things people tell you that you should be doing/have to be doing, and they usually share them in the guise of giving advice or trying to help you improve your writing or story.

These rules may address everything from punctuation:

> *You should never use the Oxford comma.*
> *You should always use the Oxford comma.*

To word usage:

> *Never use adverbs.*
> *Don't write with similes.*

To story structure:

> *Prologues are bad, never use prologues.*
> *Don't open your chapter with a dream sequence.*
> *Never end your chapter with a character going to sleep.*

To pacing:

> *Your story has to open in a moment of action. It should open when the pot is boiling.*

The one thing they have in common is that they're often presented as absolutes, as non-negotiable, and seen as something that *must* be followed in your writing, suggesting that if you don't stick to them, your writing might not be up to par.

They can be comforting to new writers, because they give a structure and a formula to follow, but following every absolute, each rule shared, also can result in a voice that's being stifled and a story that doesn't get to be fully creatively developed.

While I tend to speak of these rules in a very hyperbolic way, that's more for effect and impressing upon authors how important it is to understand their own voice and style.

Instead, I encourage authors, especially new authors, to think of the pieces of advice people give you as tools in your writer's toolkit. They can help you shape your story and improve your craft, but they shouldn't stifle your unique voice or creativity.

It's important to remember that there's no ultimate authority on writing (not even me, haha).

Everyone's journey is different, and what works for one person might not work for another. So, use writing rules as a starting point, but don't be afraid to bend or break them to suit your style and the story you want to tell. Your voice and the reader experience are what truly matter in the end.

There are no rules

Throughout this series of books, I try to go to great lengths to make sure you understand several basic things about my philosophy of writing. Among these basics are:

- Going through your manuscript and just applying every lesson, along with every writing "rule" you've ever been told isn't effective editing. *Sorry!*
- It's important to have a base understanding of what people say are writing "rules" because it can help you gain insight into your own writing.
- But following arbitrary writing rules isn't going to make you a better storyteller, isn't necessarily going to always (or often) make your writing better, and in fact sometimes can kill your voice.
- And following writing rules to a T isn't going to be the magic solution that gains you more readers.
- Telling a great story with compelling characters? That's going to gain you more readers.
- Also, if you're imposing those "rules" on other authors in the name of critique or editing? You may have good intentions, but you know what they say about good intentions… Instead, it's time for critique partners and editors to start thinking about

how they can positively assist authors to develop better stories without setting up absolutes that don't allow for wiggle room or for the understanding of author voice, natural storytelling, and the idea that, well, readers don't care nearly as much about adverb use as editors want us to think they do!

In short, you can ask me about a writing rule, and I can tell you the good intention it's based off of, but I'm also going to tell you to throw it out the window and stop letting it live rent-free in your head.

What I *do* think is important is:

- Having a basic understanding of how language and grammar work;
- Understanding how you can use them most effectively in your own writing.
- Also understanding where certain advice, feedback or even your own choices may have a negative impact on your craft.
- Creating compelling story and characters.
- Keeping the reader experience top of mind as you edit.
- Realizing that when we talk about writing rules vs. reader experience, that doesn't mean that things like punctuation aren't important. I think punctuation is extremely important to the reading (and writing) experience. I also think good editing, cleaning up typos, and creating the best reader experience possible with attention to detail is also important.

Don't use this chapter as an excuse not to deliver a quality product to your customers!

TAKE ACTION

What's one writing rule that you've heard or that someone has tried to impose on your manuscript? Write it on a Post-it® note, scrunch it up, and throw it in the trash. Be free of that rule!

And, if you're feeling really honest, do the same for a writing "rule" that you've told someone they have to follow!

TIPS & TIDBITS

Author Question: I'm wondering too if you can suggest ways for new authors to find the right balance here and with author voice? How can someone find their style, their voice, their way of writing while also making sure it is something people want to read? How can they figure out what to take from the rule books/road maps and what to chuck out? Or is there a right stage to do this at? For instance is it better to just write their story and then worry about stuff when it comes to the editing stage?

Angela's Response: Thanks for this question.

First, to learn your author voice, you need to write. Write some more. Find the sweet spot where you actually *have* an author voice, before you worry about protecting your author voice. A lot of new authors are simply trying to figure out the mechanics of writing a story, and getting the story finished. Those first drafts, and first few books, are often fairly awkward and not always that great, because as a new author you're not comfortable enough writing to be comfortable enough to really *have* a strong, clear author voice.

What I find is that most authors dig into their voice after writing and rewriting a few books. That's when you figure out who you are as a writer and become more comfortable separating your voice and characters' voices, and making them all distinct things.

So new authors, the most important thing is really writing and rewriting and drafting and redrafting.

Once you've done that, you gain confidence in who you are as a writer and then it becomes easier to know whether a "rule" is something that works within your own way of storytelling or if it's not something you want to listen to.

In answer to this part of your question, "while also making sure it is something people want to read…" that's where getting trusted feedback comes in. Working with strong critique partners, good beta readers, and hiring editors who understand your genre and your audience, are all ways that you learn to develop a story that people want to read and a style and voice that works for your audience.

As for whether or not it's better to just write the story and then worry about some things when editing, that's a very individual decision. Some authors do best drafting first and getting the story down, then going back and revising, while filling in and making editing decisions. But some others prefer to do editing and cleaning up as they write. There's no right or wrong way, there's just what works for you as an individual author.

ADDITIONAL RESOURCES

Eff the Writing "Rules" Workshop

(See the *Edit Your Way Resources* page at angelajames.-co/resources). In this workshop, I spend time talking more about author voice, the writing "rules" and how they can negatively impact author voice, and what to do instead.

CHAPTER 8
EDITING FOR INCLUSIVITY

CONTENT WARNING

This lesson touches on subject matter that may be hurtful or traumatic, including references to murder and assault on communities of color, but also including discussions of specific microaggressions and biases, and including potentially triggering words and phrases.

Author's Note

This chapter does not come with a TL;DR at the top because of the gravity of the material and importance of giving due attention to this lesson. Making use of bullet points feels both disrespectful and flippant.

If, during this chapter, you find that any of the information I've represented here is inaccurate, please let me know. This chapter pulls from my own experience over the past decade of learning and focusing on being a better editor to all authors, and as it's an ongoing process, I continue to always be open to feedback and new information.

I also must acknowledge and credit that there are 2 sections of this (notably the example lists I offer later in the chapter) that were created alongside others as we attempted to write a guide for editors and authors about writing for inclusivity.

That guide ended up never seeing the light of day, but the content was incredible and I'm sorry no one will ever see it in its entirety. It was several years' work, and the majority of the members of that team were writing from places of lived experience. Their dedication to helping others change and understand was whole-hearted, and they expended considerable emotional energy in the process.

Though the majority of this chapter is my own words and creation, it's because of them that it can exist at all, because of the amount of learning I experienced while working with them.

Their impact on my work shaped everything that came during and after, and I'm forever grateful for the changes they brought to me. It's for that reason that I will never see our time creating that guide as "wasted" even though no one will ever get to see it as the company ultimately decided not to utilize it.

Equity and Inclusivity

As I wrote the original version of this lesson for *Before You Hit Send®* in 2021, six Asian women were shot and killed in a hate crime. When I was updating the information in 2022, Derek Chauvin had just been convicted of the murder of George Floyd, and an hour later a young Black girl, Ma'Khia Bryant, was shot and killed by police.

In 2023, the week I was again updating this section, Ralph Yarl, a sixteen-year-old Black child had been shot twice by an older white man simply for knocking on his door in a moment of getting the wrong address when picking up his younger brothers from a friend's house.

These are U.S.-centric examples, but this isn't a uniquely American issue. We've seen the same patterns —police killings, systemic bias, dehumanizing rhetoric —play out from France to Brazil to Australia. The language we use everywhere shapes who we see as human.

Why do I tell you this?

Because while this section is ostensibly about reading for inclusivity and being aware of racial biases, it is also imperative, now, at this moment, as well as moving forward into the future, to center the importance of racial equity not just in books and in publishing, but in life.

We must work to be cognizant of biases and keep at the forefront the realization of how insidiously microaggressions and potentially harmful phrasing can creep into fiction writing, as well as other aspects of publishing—and life.

We also need to understand that this marginalizing language might feel as if it's "no big deal" in works of fiction, but in fact, those small grains of sand can add up to building a desert without human empathy, compassion, fairness and accessibility.

So those small grains of sand need to be removed as

much as possible, so as not to provide a place for inaccessibility, dehumanization, superiority and hate to live and grow.

————

I must also start by saying I am not an expert on reading or writing for inclusivity and will never present myself as an expert, because I'm like many of you, a traveler on a long path of learning and growth, a path that continues as the world changes.

But I realized several years ago that it would be absolutely remiss to host a course on editing and not talk about this. And the same holds true of offering a book on editing. So I've worked to get this information into the book in a way that you can immediately take action and implement changes in your own writing, and you can continue your learning through additional resources.

As with the other topics, I will not go in depth into this topic, as that would be impossible.

This chapter will be one of overview and suggestions, things to start your journey in thinking about this (if you haven't already) and an idea of what to start being aware of. Throughout the chapter, as well as at the end, I am also going to provide a list of resources to check out from people who are doing this work and who you should definitely listen to!

At its heart, this topic is also about being aware of and confronting our own privilege. While far beyond the scope of this book, it is still necessary to mention, because our privilege is most frequently what keeps us from understanding why something is harmful or from recognizing the problematic nature of certain writing choices.

Definitions

Let's start with some definitions, so we all come from the same basis of understanding. For this, because as I mentioned, I am not presenting myself as a DEI (Diversity, Equity, and Inclusion) expert, I'm going to provide some resources as well as my basic definitions. The first line of each definition shows you how these three words are different—they are not interchangeable.

Diversity is the way in which each individual differs from each other. It includes a number of different considerations and characteristics, including (but not limited to) race, religion, ethnicity, gender, as well as sexual orientation, socioeconomic status, culture, weight, disability, physical characteristics, and other ways in which people may differ from one another.

Using myself as an example, I may differ from others in that I'm an overweight white woman with ADHD who's an atheist.

In an article by Meg Bolger that I've listed on the resource page, she points out that an individual is not diverse, but an individual is instead a unique unit. She puts emphasis on the fact that something is diverse only *in comparison* to other things in the collective or group. Using diverse to refer to an individual has actually become targeted coded language, a euphemism, if you will, that suggests something is outside the "social norm" (and that is something we want to avoid in best writing practices). So when talking about diversity, you really aren't referring to an individual (and you don't want to refer to an individual as "diverse"), you're referring to a group of individuals, and how they compare to one another in terms of different elements and characteristics.

Equity refers to the ongoing process of identifying and dismantling barriers so individuals from marginalized identities can access the same opportunities and resources as others.

Unlike equality, which treats everyone the same, equity seeks to achieve fairness by recognizing that different people face different obstacles—and addresses those differences through systemic change, targeted support, and resource redistribution. Equity is achieved not by ignoring differences, but by addressing them.

Inclusion is the intentional practice of creating environments where all people—especially those from historically excluded identities—are not only present, but have the power, opportunity, and agency to shape, participate in, and thrive within systems, organizations, and communities.

An example of this in the Before You Hit Send course this book is based on could be the different ways in which we deliver content (text, video, audio and worksheets), so people can choose different forms of learning and also have individual accessibility options.

Want to dive more in depth on DEI and what it means? Read the article referenced earlier by Meg Bolger (see the *Edit Your Way Resources* page at angelajames.co/resources), this is a great starting point. I've also included additional resources at the end of this chapter.

Since this is a huge topic with a lot of work and learning to be done, and we can't cover it all, in this chapter I'm going to focus on three key topics in fiction writing:

1. Microaggressions and harmful content
2. Writing white as default
3. Are you the right writer for this story or character?

Microaggressions

Microaggressions are those remarks, derogatory word use, actions, and questions that happen often casually in writing and everyday interactions, which create harm and pain to the recipient, because they are specific to a person's individual identity and groups to which they belong. They often play into stereotypes, and while may be unintentional, do harm because they perpetuate discriminatory thinking and behavior.

Dr. Derald Wing Sue, who has written several books on the subject of microaggressions, defines them as: "The everyday slights, indignities, put-downs, and insults that people of color, women, LGBT populations, or those who are marginalized experience in their day-to-day interactions with people."

Dr. Wing Sue goes on to explain how they can show up seemingly hidden: "Microaggressions often appear to be a compliment but contain a meta-communication or a hidden insult to the target groups in which it is delivered. People who engage in microaggressions are ordinary folks who experience themselves as good, moral, decent individuals. Microaggressions occur because they are outside the conscious awareness of the perpetrator."

I would presume that most of you reading this book would find you identify yourself as a "good, decent individual", but it's important to remember that because microaggressions are very often learned, ingrained, and unconscious, it takes active work to seek them out and eradicate them.

Most of us have said or written microaggressions, through use of phrasing, questions, and words, and the only way to be aware of microaggressions is to listen, learn, and read what those from marginalized communities are saying.

What do microaggressions look like in writing?

Microaggressions in writing can look very similar to what microaggressions look like in everyday life.

One good example is having a character make a joke at the expense of another. Perhaps you have a male character in an office setting who arranges a golf outing but tells his female co-worker she can go shopping while the men golf. Or maybe a character "jokes" about an Asian accent. "Flied lice" for instance.

But, you may be thinking, "it's just a joke". That phrase is actually a great indication that something is a microaggression and harmful/hurtful to the group it's directed at.

Stereotypes and clichéd characters are another common microaggression. In writing, this can look like including Black characters whose only role is to be a magical guide (for example, the "magical negro" stereotype), or who are presented as caricatures such as the Angry Black Woman, Spicy Latina, Dragon Lady, Sassy Gay Friend, or even Crazy Cat Lady (for further reading, see the article in the resource list on the "Mammy" stereotype), or who only have roles of servitude or walk-on/walk-off roles but no character development.

Using LGBTQ+ characters only as support characters is another example. "Sassy gay friend" is an acknowledged harmful and repeated stereotype.

A number of harmful microaggressions were seen in news outlets after the 2021 shooting of six Asian women in Atlanta, GA.

- Many news outlets did not list the women's full names, but rather truncated them and left off parts of their names, presuming/assuming a white default of middle names rather than researching to understand that these were their full names, as they should be referenced: Daoyou Fen,

> Xiaojie Tan, Delaina Hyun Jung Grant,
> Suncha Kim, Soon Chung Park, Yong A. Yue.

- News outlets perpetuated in using the term "massage parlor" in reports of the shooting. This is a highly racialized (and often fetishized) term.
- Depictions of Asian women as "meek" or "submissive" or "hypersexual" in regard to their behavior and their work.
- And while perhaps not specifically related to that shooting, Donald Trump referring to COVID as the "China virus" creates an ongoing anti-Asian sentiment of hate.

Why do we not realize something is a microaggression?

Lack of awareness occurs by not doing research, by not reading articles, and not following a broad scope of humans on social media and communities, in order to better understand viewpoints, cultures, lived experiences, languages, customs and other things that aren't within your own everyday life.

No one is immune from using microaggressions, me included. In the *Before You Hit Send®* course, in the past, there have been some lessons that have contained harmful phrases or sentences.

For instance, in original versions of this course, I used the terms hero/heroine, rather than referring more broadly to protagonists or main characters. Many years past, in a lesson on dialogue, I had a section titled "Make your men sound like men." Oof. That is an incredibly harmful and hurtful microaggression that makes a lot of stereotypical assumptions.

It is these things that can seem "small" because perhaps we've grown used to our default language, but that can exclude and hurt readers. It's these things that we have to work to recognize in our own use. We should also utilize editors, critique partners and sensitivity readers to point out those things that we miss and need assistance rooting out of our work.

Additional examples of how microaggressions may appear in writing and everyday life:

- A character refusing to learn the correct pronunciation of someone's name and giving them a nickname instead.
- A character using inappropriate humor that degrades a specific person or an entire marginalized group (e.g., joking about the local Chinese restaurant serving dog).
- A character complimenting a non-white character on their "good English."
- "Where are you from?"
- "What are you?"
- "You're not like other…women/gay men/Black people I've met before."
- "I always forget you're a…woman/gay man/Black person."
- "You're so good looking…for a dark-skin

girl/an overweight person/someone in a wheelchair."
- "You don't act gay."
- Nonverbal: locking your doors when you see a Black man, clutching your purse tighter when a person of color gets near you.
- "I'd hate to be you," said to a disabled person.
- "Because we're all women here…" (assuming someone's gender).
- Portraying a female secondary character as a terrible person because they…have sex with men/dress more provocatively/wear a lot of makeup.
- Always portraying the antagonist as "other" or "different." (A character of a racially/ethnically marginalized community, a character from the LGBTQ+ community, etc.)
- When talking about/to a gay couple, "Who's the man in the relationship?"
- Using food to describe skin tone.
- "All Lives Matter." (This phrase deprioritizes and erases the critical needs of specific, vulnerable communities.)

When looking for bias and microaggressions in your writing, pay close attention to the following list of editorial points, which are especially subject to unintentional bias:

- Characterization of the protagonist/hero/heroine.
- Characterization of the antagonist/villain (especially concerning stereotypes).
- How you're using secondary and tertiary characters.
- Frequency and description of marginalized groups.
- Historically problematic words and phrases.
- Potentially problematic themes.
- Tropes with biased or bigoted origins (tvtropes.org is a good resource to check!).
- Plot points that reinforce problematic perspectives.
- Stereotypical interactions between marginalized characters.

Problematic Words and Phrases

Microaggressions go hand in hand with problematic word and phrase usage and there are a lot of them that can sneak in. During edits, I often find myself Googling words and phrases to understand the etymology and whether it's problematic, so it can be flagged. Here's a list of a few examples that you may have used yourself. If you're interested in the background of these, it's easily found via an internet search and worth researching:

- "Gypped," "gypsy"
- "Uppity"
- "Oriental"

- "Crazy," "psycho"
- "Dumb blonde," "bimbo"
- "Spaz"
- "Lame"
- "Midget"
- "Indian giver"
- "Ghetto"
- "Jewed down"
- "Retarded"
- "Fucktard"
- "OCD"
- "Exotic"
- "Blackball," "blacklist"
- "Tribe"
- "Spirit animal"
- "Peanut gallery"
- "Thug"
- "Savage"

Writing White as Default

Writing white as default is something most white authors do with no conscious realization. Simply put, white as default is when you presume that a character being white (and likely also non-disabled, cisgender, and heterosexual) is the "normal" and therefore the baseline upon which all characters are written.

This results in you only describing things such as skin color, disability, sexuality when the character is not "default." In other words, you may make it a point to note that a person has brown skin, but you don't ever reference a white person's skin color / description.

This is a significant form of "othering" in fiction and one that creates a situation in which you, the author, describe characters only in order to point out how they're "different" or "other." But you do not do the same for the "default" because you unconsciously assume that the reader will read them as white, non-disabled, cisgender, and heterosexual.

Recognizing whether you're writing white as default is really not that difficult once you begin critically examining your character descriptions and make note of who you're describing and how you're describing them.

Further reading (links found on the Edit Your Way Resources page):

- "Dismantling the White Default"
- "Waiting for the day that Characters Don't Default to White"
- "White is not the Default: Confronting White Bias in Books"

Are You the Right Writer for This Story or Character?

I'm not here to tell you that you can't write a character outside your experience or culture. However, what I am going to ask you to ask yourself is if you're the right person to tell that story.

I don't know the answer.

I don't think the answer, though, is to never write characters who aren't exactly like you, because while that may feel "easy," it doesn't feel representative of the world in which we live.

So what's an author to do?

Research. Learn. Listen. *Read*. Ask questions (of yourself and others). Do the hard work to give authentic, accurate, and sensitive portrayals and to begin to more naturally write inclusively.

There are a lot of considerations to take into mind when deciding to write a protagonist outside of your own experience. You do need to ask if you're able to accurately and authentically portray them.

Ask yourself, are you telling the story in place of someone who's been historically blocked from telling their own story, and therefore taking their place? Are you committed to doing the research and getting input from those with the lived experiences you're writing about? What will your process be for ensuring you tell the story through the appropriate lens?

A Few Tips for Writing Marginalized Characters

Here are some tips on writing marginalized characters that I learned from that team I previously mentioned working with:

1. **Research is key.** If you're writing or editing a character with a different background than your own, start by reading the works of authors who have written such books successfully. Aim to read as many primary sources as possible.

2. **Talk with people in the community you're writing about.** Learn the nuances of that community's experience and understand that, as in any group, contradictions in perspective and experience frequently exist. Ask yourself what these contradictions suggest about the marginalized characters you plan to create.

3. **Create well-rounded characters.** A rule of thumb when writing any kind of character, but even more important when writing outside your experience. Avoid characterizations that hinge on one specific trait. Never make ethnicity, sexuality, disability, or any other minority status the most interesting thing about a character. Strive for nuanced characters that are fully realized, and stories that get at the universal through the specific.

4. **Vet your book.** Getting feedback from a diverse set of critique partners or hiring sensitivity readers can help you ensure you're writing marginalized characters thoughtfully. Take every reader's notes into consideration along with your own research and your editor's feedback, and edit accordingly. And note that members of the same marginalized groups may have different experiences and opinions on what is accurate or false, helpful or harmful. Not every person will agree on everything, and there may be conflicting viewpoints.

5. **It's okay to get it wrong in the first draft.**
Allow yourself the freedom to make mistakes, including cultural mistakes, in your first draft. Again, no one will know every single detail about every single different community, and if you get something wrong you can fix it in revisions. You just need to be willing to make edits! Gather feedback from a diverse group of readers and address cultural mistakes as you revise.

If you're committed to writing protagonists outside your experience, as well as to writing with a thoughtfulness toward inclusion and diversity, I cannot recommend the Writing the Other workshops and book highly enough. The workshops from the Writing the Other team are presented on an ongoing manner from a variety of presenters from a range of backgrounds and lived experiences. You may wish to subscribe to their newsletter as new workshops are released frequently and cover a range of subjects.

Sensitivity Readers

Sensitivity readers may also be referred to as diversity or authenticity readers.

Because authors ask about sensitivity readers often, I feel I do need to include a short section here to describe what a sensitivity reader may do. I do not offer advice on hiring or using these readers.

I also think it's important to note that the term "sensitivity reader" itself is a much discussed and contentious one and as with many of the topics, there is no consensus of agreement on either the phrase or use of these readers.

Sensitivity readers are those who have experience in reading for authenticity and lived experiences. There are two categories of readers in this area:

- Sensitivity readers who read for an overview in order to give feedback on potential problematic content, descriptions, and words;
- Sensitivity readers who are from a specific identity or lived experience and who are reading specifically for those lived experiences.

Though you may employ a reader, it's important to remember a few things:

1. This is not a fail-safe and the onus still lies with you, the author, to do the work.
2. There is no "one voice" in any group, so what one reader may not flag, another may find problematic.
3. Groups of any kind are not homogenous, with homogenous identities and thoughts, so do not think that hearing from one person in a group reflects the opinions, thoughts, or feelings of all (or even many).

Further reading (links found on the Edit Your Way Resources page):

- "What Sensitivity Readers Actually Do"
- "How 'sensitivity readers' are changing the publishing ecosystem—and raising new questions about what makes a great book "
- "Literary Color Lines: On Inclusion in Publishing"
- "What the Job of a Sensitivity Reader is Really Like"

A Few Final Thoughts

This has always been the hardest topic for me to cover in *Before You Hit Send*® and now in this book, because while I am writing and teaching from a place of expertise when talking about writing and editing, I'm still on a journey of understanding how to best represent diversity, equity and inclusion in fiction.

So this has been a chapter that has stretched me, made me sit with my own discomfort, and more than once questioned my ability to write it.

Much, I assume, like many of you feel about tackling characters outside of your own lived experiences.

Even during the beta read portion of this book, several of the beta readers asked if I would please expand this section to explain how to do all of this, how to gain a level of comfort, how to make it easier.

One of my readers said, "I could see authors reading this section and just deciding to never write outside their own identity so they won't risk doing harm. I'm not really sure how you fix that, but I leave this chapter feeling tired and scared of making a mistake instead of feeling empowered to make a difference in this area by considering the weight of my words and making deliberate choices or..."

That's an incredibly vulnerable and honest thing to share, and I'm sure they're not alone in feeling that way, and they're not wrong that that will be the takeaway for some authors.

So how do I empower you to move forward? One thing has been underlying this whole chapter but let me maybe state it super, super plainly:

You have to listen to, learn from, research, and seek out people who aren't just like you. Do the hard work. Do the research. Ask questions. Be present.

And, as I was editing this, I was gifted some feedback with this amazing tool to also include and use:

SEEK TO UNDERSTAND

Ask questions and don't respond.
You're not looking for engagement, not opening a debate, you're seeking to understand. Clarify, don't confront.

One of the notes that I include in all of my edit letters is a reminder that we all have different lived experiences, and I'm not here to question anyone's lived experiences—I may not know your background and experiences, so I *will* include editorial questions about them, but if those are your experiences, I also know that it's not up for debate.

So as you seek to understand, also remind yourself that people aren't obligated to share their lived experiences with you, but when they do, that's a gift, and isn't up for you to debate.

Why am I not telling you exactly what to do and how to do it? Because not only am I not the right person to do that, there isn't one right way. It's going to depend on your unique situation and your unique book.

Instead, this chapter is meant to provide some foundation and set you up for your next steps, and those next steps aren't going to be ones that I can just lay out in this chapter. Those next steps are found in the additional resources I'm sharing, in your ongoing learning, and the variety of people you connect with, ask questions of, and hire.

I think trepidation, caution, and fear are healthy because they'll encourage you to do it well. If you just decide not to do it, well, that's its own choice but it would be the same as if I hadn't included this chapter in this book, and had taken the path of least resistance and just ignored the topic.

This chapter didn't come easily for me, it took hours, weeks, months, years to learn enough to write it, and it required me to reach out to many different people and sources for support, insight, information and critique.

And that's how it's going to work for you. You can do it. No, it won't be easy. But it will make a difference.

TAKE ACTION

As I mentioned, there's not enough room in this chapter, and I don't have enough expertise to tell you "do it exactly like this" but I can give you some ideas of a few places to start as well as a few things to consider.

This is just the beginning of the work involved in writing inclusively.

One way to start implementing is to pay attention to whether you're writing white as the default. Are you only describing the non-white characters? Go through your book and look at your character descriptions—who are you describing, how are you describing them, and what are you pulling readers' attention to?

Also notice: are you only writing white characters or are your non-white characters only in non-important, temporarily on-page roles? Are you depending on stereotypes to fill in characteristics of your non-white or LGBTQ+ characters?

Other things you can do:

- Visit Appendix E at the back of this book and use The Heart Test provided by Kharma Kelley.
- Spend some time with your thoughts and decide on one thing that you can implement or look for in your work to begin writing and editing for inclusivity.
- Give yourself space to absorb and learn, but also don't pass this lesson by as "too hard"!
- Read widely and inclusively.

- Diversify your social media consumption—choose how you engage, but focus on how you're listening and learning, and who you're listening and learning from.
- When the conversation isn't about you, listen, don't insert yourself into conversations unnecessarily.
- Be open to change within yourself and be willing to *do the work*. What does that mean? It can include doing things from this list, but also being willing to hold yourself accountable, catching yourself when you get defensive (you will get defensive), or doing the hard work of unlearning harmful behaviors (start with catching yourself when you use certain words or phrases, and unlearning those from your vocabulary).
- If an apology is called for, what work and learning will you do to make sure it doesn't happen again? Don't make excuses, but own your mistake, and be clear with what changes you're making or what learning you're doing so it doesn't happen again. Then actually do the work to implement those changes.

ADDITIONAL ACTIVITY

Quick note:

I recognize that the use of AI can be in itself problematic. However, I'm suggesting using AI here because one thing we all need to be careful of is how we impose on other people's time and energy, including their emotional energy.

Expecting our friends and acquaintances to do the work by educating us is a demand and a microaggression of its own, so using other tools and resources available to us is important.

———

Enter this into your AI tool (ChatGPT, Claude, etc.):

I'm writing a fiction book with a [insert description] character. What are some microaggressions or harmful descriptions I should watch out for?

For example:

I'm writing a fiction book with a Korean secondary character. What are some microaggressions or harmful descriptions I should watch out for?

And as follow-up questions:

Any specific descriptors to avoid?
Can you recommend books by Korean or Korean American authors that should read?

You can ask the AI other questions that are specific to what you're writing.

** *Please remember that using AI to assist you in this*

*way does NOT replace lived experience, whether it's
yours or someone else's, so please don't think that just
because you used AI, your book is totally unproblem-
atic. This is just one more tool for you to use!*

STYLE NOTE

Over the past few years, I've shifted my style several
times as to how to capitalize Black and white, based on
major industry style guide recommendations as well as
input from many different voices. For a time, I capitalized both, following a sensitivity reader's recommendation and the guidance that felt right at the time. But
language evolves, and so does our understanding of it.

Subsequently, in this book, I've chosen to capitalize
Black and lowercase white. After a comment left by the
DEI expert I hired to give me feedback on Edit Your
Way, in which she commented that "choosing to capitalize 'White' is a choice to racialize" and that this
choice is fine, but one I must make consistently, I went
on a journey of understanding what this meant.

Ultimately, I decided not to capitalize white. And in
the interest of transparency, and of showing that our
choices can change as we learn, I want to share that
decision with you here.

I'd understood that capitalizing Black acknowledges
a shared cultural and historical identity. What I didn't
fully understand was that keeping white lowercase
avoids turning whiteness into a parallel cultural label
or giving it weight it doesn't need. As I was told,
choosing to capitalize white is a choice to racialize it; to
frame whiteness as a distinct identity group rather than

as the unmarked social position it has historically occupied.

That's not a neutral act. And for me, it's important that this work reflects not just grammatical preference, but awareness of power, privilege, and how language shapes both.

So my choice is not to capitalize white because doing so would racialize it, turning whiteness into a defined identity group. The goal isn't to maintain it as a default, but to avoid centering it or giving it undue prominence.

ADDITIONAL RESOURCES

A non-exhaustive list of recommended resources, in addition to those already in the chapter, is available on the *Edit Your Way Resources* page at angela-james.co / resources.

SECTION TWO
BUILDING YOUR EDITING PROCESS

CHAPTER 9
EDIT STAGES DEFINED

I n my years as an editor at three publishing houses, mentoring dozens of freelance editors and helping them respond to authors' questions about editing, and now running my own independent editorial business, I've consistently encountered authors' confusion and lack of information over the editorial process.

What I find is that most authors don't know what they should be doing in each stage of edits (or what their editors should be doing in each stage) and it can create a frustration or overwhelm with editing, a dislike of editing, and just a general state of wondering… "How do I edit?"

This chapter is going to thoroughly (I hope!) define and explain the different stages of the editing process. I'm also going to incorporate information about what an author should expect from each stage of edits when working with an editor.

TL;DR

- Understanding the differences between the various stages of editing as well as knowing what to expect—and what not to expect—can go a long way in helping an author approach edits with less anxiety and more confidence.
- For those authors hiring their own editors, it can aid in understanding what they're paying for, what services they need and why they need them.
- There are a lot of people you can receive feedback, critique and edits from during the lifecycle of your book. Who you use and at what stage can make a difference to both your workflow and the quality of the feedback you get.
- There are generally four main stages of edits (in the order they should follow during the editing process):
  1. Developmental (aka Content) Edits
  2. Line Edits
  3. Copy Editing
  4. Proofreading

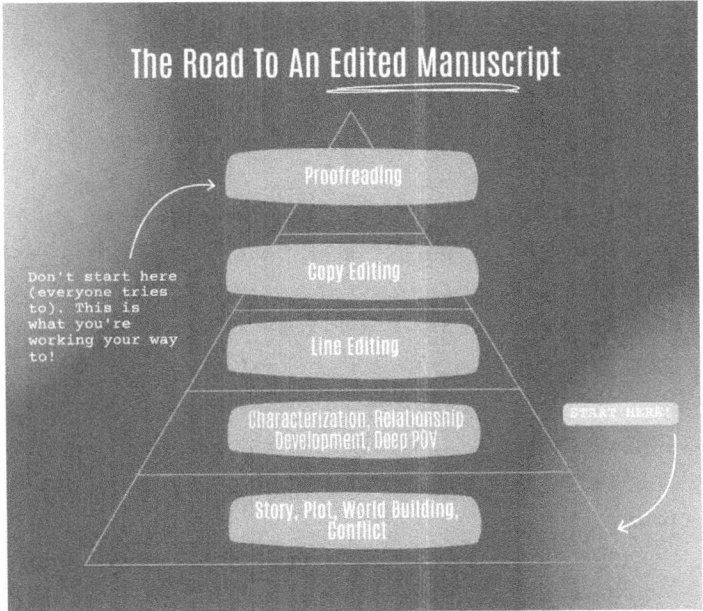

As with anything in publishing, as more and more people have entered publishing and gleaned their information from the internet, some of the terms we once used to differentiate the different stages of edits have become confused. So I'm going back to the basics and explaining how traditional publishing has long defined the different stages of editing, and how I've defined them over my years teaching authors about editing.

There are four stages of editing, and I'm listing them in the order you would want to approach them in your editing process:

1. Developmental Edits
2. Line Editing
3. Copy Editing
4. Proofreading

This chapter will also touch briefly on several other "stages" that some authors use, including beta readers, alpha readers, and sensitivity readers (sometimes also called diversity or authenticity readers).

At a publishing company, these stages may be called different things, or there may be additional rounds of edits behind the scenes you may not even see, as there are edits for formatting and proofing errors post type-setting.

The information in this chapter is meant as an overview to familiarize new authors with the editorial process, but this process may look slightly different depending on the publisher or editor. It may look even more different for those working with freelance editors, depending on the author's budget, what edits the editor and author have agreed to, and time constraints.

I have also seen some misuse of terminology (calling copy edits, line edits is a very common misuse of terms) so you will need to dig into conversation with your editor before hiring them, or working with them, to ensure you're getting the level of edits you need.

Why is knowing the distinction between each stage important? Because having this foundation allows you to:

1. Set your expectations when working with an editor—know what they mean when they say

> they do certain types of edits, and know what
> you should be able to expect from them in
> terms of results.
> 2. Understand the basic editing process.
> 3. Set up a reasonable editing process for
>   yourself.

―――――

DEVELOPMENTAL EDITS

Also called: Content Edits, Substantive Edits, Story Edits, Big Picture Edits, Structural Edits, Conceptual Edits.

This is the first stage of editing, and I do mean the first stage. Before you start worrying about commas, or thinking about sentence structure, your story is your primary concern in edits.

This is the stage that your readers most care about, because while your commas may put the polish on, no reader ever finished a story and said, "Wow, I really loved the use of the well-placed commas in that book."

Your readers are looking to be transported by your plot, fall in love with your characters, be held in suspense by your mystery, and be given a story that makes them want to spend their time with it as it unfolds.

Developmental edits are the magic that helps you get there. I often say that writing is for the author and editing is for the reader, and it's the most true in this stage of edits.

Here is where you dive into the meat and heart of the story. This stage is what we'd call the overview, story, or content pass because you and/or your editor are looking at the big picture of your book.

And if you're working on developmental edits with an editor, a skilled professional editor is also someone who can think about more than just the story as the story. They can partner with an author to discuss the author's goals for the book, how it fits into their brand, offer insight into the market and marketability of the book, advise on an on-brand cover and cover copy, and work with the author to achieve a polished product.

In developmental edits, you're going to be working on:

- Plot
- Characterization
- Conflict (internal and external)
- Relationship development (whether a romantic relationship, friendships, familial relationships or other)
- Pacing
- Deep point of view (POV)
- World-building
- Story—which encompasses many of these elements but also things such as mystery development, suspense or thriller aspects
- Story continuity and consistency
- ...and more

A thorough developmental edit (and good developmental editor) will also be on the lookout for microaggressions, bias, representation, stereotypes, diversity, and inclusion in the book content, world-building, and characterization.

Developmental edits are my absolute favorite stage of edits and this is where the real magic happens. This is where you, as the author (and/or editor) can figure out what's missing, what needs to change, how to build, repair, layer in, remove and add.

In developmental edits, your goal is to create the story you want to read, and your readers didn't know they wanted.

Edits will (should) focus on how the *reader* experiences all aspects of the story, from beginning to end, including prologue, epilogue and everything in between, and should be aiming to achieve reader satisfaction by telling a compelling story with all of the elements tightly woven together and fully developed characters that remain memorable for the reader.

These edits are what makes the reader fall in love with the story, characters, world, and what makes them recommend your book.

The developmental edits stage is where the bulk of your time in edits should be spent as this is the most crucial stage and one that should never be skipped.

LINE EDITS

The line editing stage generally takes place after developmental edits, but it can also happen in tandem with minor dev edits. This is the stage where you or your line editor—who may be a different editor than your developmental editor but may also be the same person—will be focusing on craft in a more detailed way.

Comments on story elements can still happen during this round, but these edits are primarily focused on how your prose is written. In this stage, an editor may rewrite a sentence if it's an objective fix or to demonstrate an alternative phrasing, but the author's voice should never be overwritten.

A good editor will give the author room to revise and learn how to use their authorial voice, not the editor's. A good editor also isn't looking to impose a bunch of nonsense writing "rules" on an author; rather, this editor is working to improve craft in a way that's natural to the story, the author's voice and culture.

I have seen line edits sometimes called copyedits but the two stages, while having overlap, are different stages and line editing comes before copy editing.

Line editing is where the focus on the actual craft of putting words and sentences together happens. This stage focuses on the readability and almost the flow of the reading.

While in line editing, you may have some overlap with the previous stage of developmental editing, and the next stage of copy editing, *your focus is on structure and writing craft*. Here you and the editor will be determining some of your author style and looking to enhance and preserve both author and character voice.

Some of the elements that may be included are:

- Author and character voice
- Use of action and dialogue tags

- How you're using punctuation for voice impact (for instance, commas, excessive exclamation marks, parentheses, em dashes, etc.)
- You're also going to be covering style things like word choices and word repetition
- Repetitive or confusing sentence structure
- Overuse of words and sentence structure
- Awkwardly phrased sentences
- Use of contractions
- Point of view slips
- Tense errors
- Misplaced modifiers
- Dangling participles
- Incorrect word usage
- Other line-specific craft work

Interestingly, though I generally talk about deep point of view as something done in the developmental editing stage, the line editing stage is often where just as much work on deep POV happens!

In the early stages of your writing career, line editing may be heavier as you learn to write and how to structure your writing for the most impact and the least intrusion into the reader's experience. As you write more, line editing almost always decreases and is often less and less necessary for a more experienced author with an established voice.

This stage is also where editor interference with author voice is most common. This is the stage where editors are most likely to simply rewrite phrasing, make wholesale changes, rather than suggestions, and put things into what sounds best *to them* rather than what is natural to the author's voice and writing.

This is not to say all line editing is an interference with author voice, because it's absolutely not, but this is the stage where editors are most likely to struggle with trying to impose writing "rules" and their ideas of structure and phrasing on the author.

This is the stage where the author may most want to sample the editor's work in advance, or ask them questions about how they edit.

COPY EDITS

Also called: Final Line Edits.

Though this is the stage many authors find it easiest to default to starting with (due to their more objective nature), copy edits are actually the third stage of edits that take place once all content and line edits have been addressed. At this stage, the book is past the rewrite stage and is entering the polishing stage to become production-ready.

Copy edits are done by a completely different editor —not the developmental editor and not the line editor. You want someone coming into the copy editing stage with completely fresh eyes, seeing the book for the first time and seeing what's actually on the page without all of the previous iterations and story details floating around in their head.

This will allow them to catch inconsistencies and

wrong story details in a way someone who's already seen the book multiple times will be unable to do.

Copy edits should not occur until the developmental and line edit stages are complete, as the copy edit stage is moving the book toward final completion, and major changes shouldn't occur at this stage or beyond.

The book moves to copy edits when the author and editor feel they've revised the story for the best possible reading experience and are now ready to move on to the polishing stages.

In copy edits, the editing is moving to more of a micro or granular level of editing, and the changes both here and in the proofreading stage are going to be more on the objective versus subjective level.

What I mean by that is that there's less "guessing" or "figuring out" things at the copy edit and proofreading level because there are guides to follow, whereas in the developmental and line edit stages, the author and editor are utilizing more intuitive or subjective skills and suggestions.

In copy edits and proofreading is where author style and style guides will most strongly come into play, and where changes will be made based on those guides, as well as based on grammar, spelling, and other standardization.

Things this stage will address are:

- Timeline and continuity errors
- Grammar
- Spelling
- Punctuation
- Correct word usage and repetition

- Detail continuity (i.e. name spelling, hair color, location)
- Fact checking (and accuracy)
- …and more

Copy edits are sometimes considered a bit pedantic as copy editors may ask questions like, "Your character is drinking iced tea from a mug but usually iced tea is in a glass, is this what you intended?"

In truth, a great copy editor can be an excellent partner on your editing team, especially if you use them for more than one book, as they learn your style, voice, series and character details.

A great copy editor (and a thorough copy edit) can save you from embarrassing gaffes and laugh-out-loud mistakes.

PROOFREADING

Also called: Mechanical Edits, sometimes Final Page Proofs.

The proofreading stage is the *final* step of the manuscript editing process after all other editing and formatting have been done.

Let me be clear: don't start working on proofreading (or even copy editing) until you've first addressed developmental and line edits because you will find that if you start here, you end up fixing things that are later deleted or rewritten anyway!

Proofreading is a very micro-detail-oriented stage of

the editorial process, and the proofreader is going to be looking at your manuscript on a granular level. This and copy edits are where you'll get the most references to things like Chicago Manual of Style and Merriam-Webster's Dictionary.

This stage may include several different passes of proofreading or more than one proofreader. At some publishers, one proofreader will read for polish and errors, and then the document will be formatted and proofread again, this time with special attention paid to formatting (or mechanical) errors. However, these can also be combined into one pass/stage/editor.

At the proofreading stage, the book is DONE. There's no more story, plot, or big detail changes to be made. There is no rewriting or rearranging of sentences unless a messy, unreadable sentence is caught, and reviewing the edits the proofreader does at this stage is often the most simple stage to review, as it's mostly yes/no decision making.

As mentioned above, the proofreader will be looking for the micro details, the typographical and mechanical errors, the small things that all of the previous editors missed, and giving a final polish. If you skip the line and/or copy editing stages, the proofreader may pull in some of the items generally found in line and copy edits as well, but the proofreading stage is meant to be the lightest stage of edits, so skipping those other stages isn't recommended unless you're an extremely detail-oriented and clean writer, or you're just incredibly strapped for money *(in which case, please don't pay a proofreader while expecting them to also carry the weight of the line and copy editors).*

Excellent proofreaders have a knowledge of style guides and grammar or punctuation standards, and a keen eye for detail. While they are reading the story, they're not editing for any story or line editing. They're editing for micro detail.

OTHER POTENTIAL STAGES OF EDITING

Some authors may also wish to include the following stages in their editing process.

Critique Partners and Writing Groups

Critique Partners

Also called: CPs, Writing Partners, Beta Readers (though this isn't quite accurate).

Critique partners are fellow writers who exchange manuscripts and provide focused, detailed feedback on each other's work. This is a reciprocal relationship—you read for them, they read for you. The relationship works best when both partners are invested in helping each other improve and grow as writers.

A good critique partner will not just point out what's not working, but explain why it's not working and often suggest ways to fix it. They'll also point out what you're doing well, so you can lean into your strengths.

It's helpful if your CP is familiar with your genre/subgenre, but also works to become familiar with and respect your voice and how you tell your story.

Critique partnerships often develop into long-term relationships because as you work together, your CP gets to know your voice, your style, and your goals. This allows them to provide increasingly targeted and valuable feedback.

Writing Groups

Also called: Writing Circles, Critique Groups, Workshop Groups.

Writing groups bring together multiple writers who meet regularly to share work, provide feedback, and support each other's writing journeys. These can be in-person or online, and may focus on specific genres or may include writers across genres.

The group dynamic offers different perspectives on your work, which can be incredibly valuable. However, the trade-off is that you typically get less focused attention on your manuscript than you would from a dedicated critique partner.

You may also find that the writing groups you can join may be a mix of writers writing different genres, and this can result in some less-than-helpful feedback when they're not familiar with your genre.

One drawback to writing groups is that the mix of personalities and types of feedback you get may create more stress than the help they give. It's important to pay attention to how much benefit you're getting from the writing group (or even a critique partner relation-ship) versus the time and energy you're spending on it.

One of the great things about a good writing group isn't just in the critique—it's in the community. Groups not only provide the accountability and motivation, but also a sense of belonging and support, as well as a decreased feeling of isolation, since editing and writing can be lonely endeavors.

Do you need both?

No, and many people don't have either a critique partner *or* a writing group. However, the two do serve different purposes and many authors find value in having both. Your writing group might give you broad feedback and keep you motivated, while your critique partner dives deep into your manuscript and helps you polish it, with an eye toward things you're specifically struggling with.

Sensitivity Readers

Because I covered sensitivity readers in the previous chapter about editing for inclusion, I won't repeat that information here.

Instead, I'll talk just a bit more about when and why you may want a sensitivity reader to be part of your editing process.

I once read an article that described sensitivity readers as something publishers hire to "cancel-proof a book." That framing misses the point entirely. The goal of working with a sensitivity reader isn't to avoid backlash; it's to create work that reflects care, accuracy, and respect.

Sensitivity readers are not gatekeepers. They're partners—professionals who help you see what you might not from your own lived experience. Their insight adds empathy, depth, and trust to your story, which strengthens the reading experience and ultimately makes your book more sellable.

So while "cancel-proofing" might be how some people first hear about sensitivity reads, the real purpose is much more meaningful: it's about honoring the people you're writing about and the readers who will see themselves in your work

Also of note: sensitivity readers should be someone you pay for their time. This is not a person you should be asking to do the work for you for free.

Sensitivity reading involves both skill and emotional labor. These readers bring lived experience, research, and professional insight to help make your story more authentic and respectful—and that expertise deserves compensation. They're taking on the weight of helping you avoid harm while improving your work, and that's valuable labor.

Paying them is part of practicing equity and respect within the publishing community.

When hiring this reader, look for people who have lived experiences with the specific character or situation you need feedback on, and also look for people who are clear about how they'll deliver the information, what type of critique they'll provide, and if they'll provide suggestions for improvement.

If you need to hire a sensitivity reader, this is best

done either before developmental edits or during developmental edits. And I will tell you that your developmental editor will always appreciate seeing that feedback as well.

Beta Readers

Beta readers are a category of "editing" that has changed and gone through somewhat of a metamorphosis.

In general, beta readers are readers, usually fans, an author utilizes to get early feedback on a manuscript.

In the past, beta reading was done for free, usually in exchange for an early look at the book in an unedited, but not rough draft state, and perhaps a free final copy.

While people who are beta readers for free do still exist, it's also becoming more common to see authors using paid beta readers.

Sometimes I think that the role between editor and beta reader can become muddied, especially as more authors use inexpensive (often less than $100) beta readers in lieu of editing, essentially utilizing the beta reader as their editor. That said, the advantage of paying someone as your beta reader is that you can have expectations, set clearer boundaries, and manage the process more strictly.

Anytime money is being exchanged, it's much easier to have an expectation of someone versus if they're doing it for free.

However, despite this muddying of roles, I tend to still believe that those who are qualified editors (and yes, I did use "qualified" on purpose) bring additional skills and insights to the work that beta readers do not.

A quick example: I recently had a client who sent the first chapter of her work-in-progress to her beta readers. They all gave feedback that they didn't like/love the chapter or the chapter didn't work for them.

None of the beta readers were able to say why.

So my author asked me to look over the chapter and give her feedback. I also told her this didn't feel like the best start to the book—but I was also able to *articulate why* and *give suggestions* for what the first chapter should instead include.

When I'm talking to people about using beta readers versus a professional editor, I often say it like this:

Beta readers will read and tell you why they don't like the book, for themselves. They view it through the lens of what *they* like (and that's totally okay!)

An editor will read and tell you why it won't work *for your intended audience*, a wider reading audience, beyond the editor's personal preferences or thoughts, and they're able to deliver the feedback in a targeted, detailed and useful way.

Think of beta readers as readers who give personal feedback and comments, almost like a private review. They see the book usually in a semi-polished state, before the author works with a developmental editor.

I think beta readers can be a tremendous asset in an author's journey, helping get the book to a place where it's ready for an editor, but I don't believe beta readers are a substitute for a professional editor.

Alpha Readers

Alpha readers are those readers who are willing to take a look at a manuscript in a very rough-draft, unedited state to give early thoughts on the story and help the author perhaps clarify some choices or direction they're struggling with.

The alpha read is intended to help give the author direction while they're still in the midst of drafting or writing the book. They may need the alpha read because they're stuck, because they want to make sure the book is taking the right direction and will appeal to readers, or because they need advice or feedback on specific plot points before they move forward.

Both the alpha and beta read require you to be very clear with your reader about what type of feedback you need from them.

Why? A few reasons. First, because many people volunteer to be alpha and beta readers without understanding what's involved in the editing process, and those readers often don't know what's expected of them or what their role in feedback is.

Second, neither the alpha read nor the beta read are going to occur (or should occur) at a time in your editing process when getting "fix this comma" comments are going to be helpful, and continuously getting those types of comments will create more work for you, and become more time consuming in sifting through them.

You want to keep alpha and beta readers focused on specific questions you have about the story, characters, plot, etc. For example:

- How did you feel about the main character's conflict?
- Did the end of the story feel rushed?
- At what point in the book did you think you had the killer figured out? Were you right?
- Was this spot I've marked here in the comments confusing?
- Who was your favorite character?
- Did you have a favorite line that stood out? (This can be helpful for identifying marketing quotes!)

Ask your early readers to keep their feedback to particular areas, leave comments for them in the document where you have specific questions, and remind them that proofreading/copy edits will come at a later stage and won't be helpful to you at this point in your edits.

STAGES OF EDITING WORKFLOW

With all these different opportunities for feedback and edits available, what does a potential workflow look like when you're writing and editing?

This workflow will give you an idea of what the editing cycle may look like, and also give you a cycle to help plot your timeline for publication. Keep in mind that this is only a suggested workflow, as you understand your own priorities and who you need/want on your team, you will develop your own that works for you.

1. Writing the book/Work in Progress (WIP)

- While you're writing the book, you may be working with a critique partner, writing group or alpha reader.

People involved: critique partner, writing group, alpha reader.

2. First draft complete

3. Self-edit—first developmental edits and then line edits.

- Go through a round or two of self-revisions after your first draft.
- This is where you should be using your editing checklist (more on developing that is coming in the upcoming chapters).
- You may still be working with a critique partner, writing group, or alpha reader at this stage.

People involved: critique partner, writing group, alpha reader.

4. Draft nearing final

- This is where beta readers enter the editing process. After you've done developmental

and some line edits, before you dive into
copy editing and proofreading.

- You could also still be working with a critique
  partner (or sending it to your critique partner
  for the first time) at this point.
- You may want to bring a sensitivity reader on
  at this stage. It's an individual choice whether
  you want to work with a developmental
  editor first.

People involved: beta readers, critique partner,
sensitivity reader.

5. Self-edits complete

- At this stage, you've edited the heck out of
  the manuscript, you've gotten feedback from
  beta readers or critique partners and now it's
  time for professional developmental editing,
  if you're indie publishing (if you're querying,
  you would do a sensitivity read still, but then
  the rest could be only self-editing before
  querying).
- This is also the stage you may wish to engage
  a sensitivity reader if you want this to come
  after developmental edits.

People involved: developmental editor, sensitivity reader.

6. Developmental edits complete

- If you worked with a developmental editor and/or sensitivity reader and you've completed all developmental edits, now you move on to line edits (these may have happened simultaneously with the same editor).

People involved: line editor.

7. Line edits complete

- Now that line edits are complete, you're ready to move on to copy edits and proofreading.

People involved: copy editor and/or proofreader.

8. Copy edits complete

- If you worked with a copy editor, or did copy edits yourself, now you may want to format the book before moving on to proofreading.
- You may choose to format after proofreading. The advantage of formatting first is the proofreader can make comments on the formatting.

People involved: formatter.

9. Formatting complete

- Now that the book is formatted, you want to have proofreading done if you haven't already. If you skipped copy editing, you may want to proofread before formatting and then again after formatting.

People involved: proofreader.

10. Proofreading complete/Formatting complete

- The proofreading and formatting are complete and the book should be in its final form.
- This is the stage at which you send out ARCs (Advanced Reader Copies) for review.
- This stage is not meant to gather feedback for changing the book, but to build word of mouth about the book and ask people for reviews on the major platforms.
- In an ideal world, you'd send out ARCs anywhere from months to weeks in advance.

11. ARCs sent out

- Now you wait. Anticipate reviews. Feel nervous. Market in advance of release day. Highlight positive reviews.
- It's publication day!! Congratulations on your new book!

To break it down and simplify it even further, you'd be working with people in loosely this order in an indie publishing situation:

- Critique Partner/Writing Groups/Alpha Reader
- Beta Reader
- Sensitivity Reader
- Developmental Editor
- Line Editor
- Copy Editor
- Formatter/Proofreader
- ARC reviewers

If you're querying, you would go through a similar stage of edits, but you wouldn't hire anyone after the sensitivity reader stage, but would go through those stages of edits yourself, format according to querying instructions, and send to the agent and/or publisher after your final proofread.

TAKE ACTION

This is a good time to think about who's on your editorial team now and who you may want on your team in the future.

- If you have current team members, are they meeting your needs and are you happy with how you're working together?
- If you don't have current team members, start thinking about where you can ask for recommendations and where you can start doing research for the team members you want to add. A few suggestions:
    - Book Acknowledgements/Copyright pages
    - Recommendations from peers
    - Social media discussions/recommendations
- And remember, you can add team members as your business grows. So it's okay to start small and grow!
- Consider barter. If you can't afford many services right off, barter with your peers. Maybe someone is great at proofreading and you make covers. Trade services.

Create your priorities

Which team members are you prioritizing in your timeline and budget?

My suggestion is always going to be prioritizing an

experienced developmental editor, and building in time for thorough developmental edits, because this is where the biggest impact on the reader experience can be made, and story and characters are what creates reader fans!

ADDITIONAL RESOURCES:

EditMatch: The Complete Toolkit for Choosing the Right Editor

This is a super fun, low-cost product I put together to help authors figure out what traits they want in an ideal editor partner, and how to choose your editor. This toolkit includes a checklist, a few videos, a workbook and extended information on exactly what you should and should not expect from an editor in each stage of edits you hire them for.

Working with Beta Readers

This is another low-cost product I created that takes authors through the steps of working with beta readers. From how to find beta readers, how many to use, and what questions to ask them. This product includes form templates to help get you started.

TIPS & TIDBITS

Author question: Some people pay beta readers (your-self, for example). It might be helpful to at least address that. What does it mean if an editor or book coach also offers paid beta reading services? What can be expected from that versus a "real" edit or an unpaid beta reader? It's probably something the readers of this book have come across if they've done their own research. Basically, when do you pay beta readers and do you need to?

Angela's response: These are really good questions that I really didn't want to answer, lol. Because it involves a lot of "it depends" and "I don't agree with that" but I'll try.

I didn't actually pay the people who agreed to beta read for me, but instead offered a credit to my online shop. For me, personally, I felt better about utilizing someone's time and asking for feedback on a book like this that's meant to add to my business, when offering something as thanks, whether payment or a gift.

A few of my beta readers noted that they would have done it without the shop credit, but the shop credit was nice, and that it did encourage them to actually complete the beta read by the deadline.

Also, I used ten beta readers for this book, I don't recommend using that many beta readers (because it's extremely time consuming to go through all that feedback, but also at that point you're just crowdsourcing, which can be its own set of problems) but I was using my own book to test processes and theories for the beta reading product I was creating that I linked above. My general recommendation is to use 3-5 beta readers.

However, many beta readers, particularly in fiction, are fans who are offering to beta read in order to get a first, early look at a favorite author's next book, and they are very happy to do it for this reason.

As such, many of these beta readers don't expect to be paid. I would also expect most beta readers not to be trained in or skilled at giving feedback, and what you're receiving in feedback is often going to be more like an early review and less like in-depth critique or edits.

All that said, *kudos to my beta readers* because they gave me a lot more insight and feedback than I would ever have expected from beta readers—perhaps because they are all authors and know how important good critique is!

CHAPTER 10

YOUR EDITING CHECKLIST —THE MOST IMPORTANT PART OF YOUR PROCESS

D oes the thought of editing make you feel a little tired and perhaps even overwhelmed? You're not alone!

One of the most challenging and often frustrating parts of editing for many authors, especially when it's your first time doing edits, is knowing exactly what you should be doing. If you've never edited before, you may find yourself floundering and asking yourself "where do I start???"

TL;DR

- A checklist gives you a process to follow.
- I'm going to tell you how to develop your own editing checklist, but if you want a template to get you started, I have a free template in Appendix C or a more detailed, filled-in template available for purchase on my website.

- Use the checklist to help you start and finish your editing process, so you don't get stuck on one piece of editing, or focus only on quick wins.
- Don't overcomplicate your editing checklist. It can be simple.
- Edits start with developmental (content) edits. Not proofreading or copy editing.

———

Where to Create Your Editing Checklist

Where you create your own checklist is completely about your own personal preference as well as using the tools available to you. Here's a few suggestions:

- Microsoft Word or Google Docs
- Excel or Google Sheets
- Notion
- Canva

Any of these tools, as well as others I may not have listed, can work to create a repeatable/reusable checklist.

If you're someone who prefers pen and paper, then just create a checklist in a notebook!

There's no perfect or right way to do this, but instead this is all about what works for your brain, your process, and is a tool you will actually use!

How to Develop Your Own Editing Checklist

The first step in developing your own checklist is an important thing to remember:

DON'T OVERCOMPLICATE IT.

Your checklist is going to naturally grow and change with you, as you grow and change as a writer. It should be a living document that you use to guide you during edits, so you can start edits without wondering where to start or what to do next. But it should also be a living document that you add to and subtract from, as you recognize your own personal writing quirks and struggles.

So to start your checklist, especially as a brand new author, you want to use resources like this book (and subsequent books in the series), critique partner suggestions, information from courses and workshops you've taken, as well as any other information you've gathered about writing or even better, specifically *your* writing.

Your checklist can start out as just a few items:

- Where you're going to start with edits.
- What you don't want to forget to look at.
- What the very last step of editing is for you.

IMPORTANT REMINDER

Your edits should not start with the fine tuning, fiddly little things.

Edits take place in this order, whether you're an author or an editor:

1. Developmental (Content) Edits
2. Line Edits
3. Copy Edits
4. Proofreading

Your editing checklist should be written in that same order. With developmental edit items (for instance, romance development or characterization/GMC—goal, motivation, conflict) being first on your checklist and proofreading (checking formatting, final pass for punctuation and spelling) being the last items.

Here's a suggestion for your first item on your editing checklist:

- Listen to the first 2 chapters and be aware of pacing, deep point of view, character connection, world-building and story setup.

And your final item(s) on your editing checklist:

- Double-check chapter headings for consistency (spelling, capitalization, and correctly in order).
- Run spellcheck.

There's a lot of room in between those steps, and you may find yourself adding a good number of items to look for in edits, as you develop your checklist. That's because edits are something that do take time and attention to detail.

But that's also why having a checklist that gives you a map to follow can make it easier rather than trying to hold all of the information in your head.

To fill in those in-between steps, again, you can use this book series and any other information you've collected. Just keep in mind not to write in a bunch of subjective writing "rules" and apply them all to your manuscript. That's not going to be the best use of your time.

Instead, add things that you know are areas of focus for you.

For instance, you could add an item to line edits that's about looking at sentence structure, or how you use dangling participles. Or maybe you want to look at your use of dialogue tags and whether they're over the top or too redundant or even necessary at all if you want to work on incorporating more action tags and deeper point of view in place of some dialogue tags.

In copy edits, you could be paying attention to direct address commas, consistency in character details, or even standardizing the capitalization of certain words for your style guide.

During your edits, you want to focus on the areas that are going to most significantly impact your readers' experience in a positive way and help create a story that keeps the reader engaged. Keeping the reader engaged is not just developmental edits, but also smoothing out writing, using punctuation, and eradicating errors that may pull the reader from the story or disrupt the reading experience.

How to Use the Checklist You Develop

Step 1:

Get in the mindset of editing for an excellent reader experience.

Start asking yourself questions such as:

- "If I change this, will it impact the reader experience?
- Will it impact it positively or negatively?
- Does it need to be changed, or am I just procrastinating, focusing on the wrong thing or just fiddling?"

Asking these questions will help you recognize when you're making important changes that materially enhance the reading experience and when you're not.

And I really want to stress that even after 20+ years of professional editing, *I still ask myself these questions every single time I edit a manuscript* when I catch myself nitpicking!

Step 2:

Start with developmental edits and choose the thing that needs the most work (pacing, plot, characterization, world-building, etc).

- There may be more than one, but start with one.
- Focus your edits in that area from start to finish of the book.

As you gain confidence in craft and storytelling, you can address the story as a whole, but breaking it down into parts makes it easier to start for a new author.

Step 3:

Get the overall story content edited before you deliberately move on to the next stages.

I just can't stress this enough. Developmental edits are hard. It's much easier to focus on the commas than the characterization. But it's the characterization that's going to sell the book to readers. Not the commas*.

The other part of this is simple time and energy

management: you don't need to be fixing commas in a sentence that's not even going to be in the final draft anyway, once you do all the story revisions.

Therefore: Story first. Commas last.

* I'm using commas as a very reductive way of referring to the copy editing and proofreading stages. There's much more to all of this than commas and I'm sure you know that, but just in case someone takes me a little too literally...

Step 4:

Now think about line editing and craft. You've probably fiddled with some of this as you've edited content, but you're doing it deliberately now. Think about the items in line editing, how the story reads, listen to the story and get a great sense of how you write.

Step 5:

Once you've gotten to a reasonable place of happiness with the story content and craft, it's time to polish. Now you move on to copy edits, and proofreading.

Step 6:

Feeling stuck? Choose a quick win.

In the editing checklist I sell, I highlight some quick wins simply because I know sometimes our brains need them, but they are all things that should happen later in edits (in other words, the quick wins are all outside of the developmental editing stage).

Here's an example of a few things I identified as quick wins from the checklist:

- Use the visual pacing technique from my pacing workshop on your first three chapters.
- Filter words
- -ly adverbs
- Figurative language (start with searching for "like" and "as if")

Still, don't be tempted to hyper focus or only focus on the quick wins or the micro edits, because that's what's easy. And though your checklist is meant to make things less intimidating, it's not going to make this process a whole lot easier or any less hard because *you still have to do the work.*

What the checklist is meant to do is to give you some ideas for how to start and how to proceed and even where to end.

If you hyper focus on those quick wins, if you only look at those quick wins, you're probably going to miss a lot of the most important things in the editing process (like everything in developmental edits). And that's not what you want your editing process to be about.

A thorough editing process is essential for creating an excellent reader experience. Every careful revision brings you closer to a book readers will love.

Rely on Your Editing Checklist

I hope you remember that writing and editing are a journey. They're comprised of a variety of different skills, and like any other skill sets, they're going to develop the more you do them.

If at any point you find yourself getting frustrated and thinking, "I can't do this!"—that is not true. All it is, is that *you're not used to doing this.* You haven't developed your process yet. Your checklist will help you.

Rely on it. Fall back on it. Get a quick win when you need one, because a quick win does help us stay motivated.

Just remember that the more you work on your editing, the more you're going to strengthen your writing, the more you're going to be a better storyteller with each book that you write and each editorial pass that you do.

Don't get discouraged. Don't give up. You *will* get there.

TAKE ACTION

Using the Editing Checklist Template from Appendix C, start creating your personalized checklist.

- Fill in and expand your editing checklist as you read these books, but also as you perform edits on your own books.
- Update the checklist and delete what you don't need.
- Put things in order of how you'll edit.

- Identify quick wins, both so you have something to fall back on, and so if you find yourself only working on the fiddly, quick win things, you'll be able to identify that and redirect yourself.

Here's an example of a few things I identified as quick wins in the copy editing section of the template:

- Character name consistency
- Capitalization of nicknames and titles
- Run spell check
- Chapter heading consistency

ADDITIONAL RESOURCES

Book Boss® Editing Checklist

If you want a free, pre-made editing checklist that you can start with, and then adapt for your own purposes, you can also use the checklist provided in Appendix C as a starting checklist.

CHAPTER 11
WHERE TO START EDITS

TL;DR

- This chapter is all about you self-editing your own work, before you move on to querying or working with indie editors.
- Start with developmental edits, not proofreading - don't be tempted by "easy" fixes when bigger story issues need work first.
- Follow the four main editing stages in order: developmental edits, line edits, copy edits, proofreading.
- Take time between writing and editing to gain distance from your work.
- Read through your entire manuscript before diving into edits to get a big picture view.
- Focus on one major issue at a time rather than trying to fix everything at once.

- Keep notes during writing to identify trouble spots that will need attention during editing.
- Create a structured approach but adapt the process to what works best for you.
- Multiple passes at each editing stage are normal and expected.

———

Let's talk about the thing that causes writer-paralysis, leaves you spending more time cruising social media than making progress on your manuscript, and causes endless frustration. The thing that maybe can cause you to fall out of love with the story you once loved so much…

"HOW do I edit this daggone book and where the heck do I start?"

Knowing where to start and how to tackle edits is sometimes not just half the battle but the full battle, because facing these questions can bring everything to a grinding halt. So let's get you into the proper mindset and give some starting points!

The editing checklist in Appendix C is an excellent tool to have handy as you start edits, especially if you're someone who's new to editing or never worked with an editor before. That checklist can give you a road map for what comes next but also give you some easy things to check off!

Let's recap, because no matter what your editor tells you, sometimes repetition is good.

When you start edits, remember the order in which edits should take place:

Stage 1: Developmental Edits (big picture edits, pacing, story arc, plot, conflict, characterization, relationship development…).

Stage 2: Line Edits (sentence and paragraph level, look at craft, language, sentence structure, creative writing. It's not about the errors, it's about the *way* you write…).

Stage 3: Copy Edits (fact-checking, grammar, punctuation, detail consistency…).

Stage 4: Proofreading (the final polish and fine-tuning).

A note about the editing stages: Each stage may include multiple passes of that type of edit (for instance, you may do two or three stages of developmental edits). And while there may be some overlap between adjacent stages, where you do some line editing along with developmental edits, for instance, there will be minimal overlap between Stage 4 (Proofreading) and Stages 1 and 2 (developmental edits and line edits).

And, yes, you better love love love your book, because you're going to be reading it a whole lot of times!

Starting in the Right Place

I know authors sometimes want to skip editing, or shortcut it as much as possible in order to save time or rush toward a deadline or toward publication.

But the answer to saving time should never be skipping editing, because that only impacts the quality of your work, which impacts the quality of the readers' experience.

So, instead, the first step in saving yourself time is starting edits in the right place.

But, Angela, what is the right place?

Glad you asked, Author!

Let me give you the worst possible answer and then give you some ways to narrow it down:

It depends.

Arrgh, the worst! The actual worst!

But it does depend. For each of you, the process is going to look a little different so what you're going to do is start developing your process.

As you grow as a writer, your editing process will evolve and change. The editing process is a lengthy one the first few times you write and edit a book because you're growing your craft, learning your trouble spots, and figuring out where you shine. Give yourself time and room to go through this process because there's no hurry (don't rush your learning) when you're first starting out.

Those of you who are already publishing? If editing isn't going so well for you or books aren't selling or reviews are tanking your editing, you might also benefit from taking some time to go through this more lengthy editing process on a book so you can start thinking even more analytically about your work.

All of that said, when you look at the steps below, it's up to you to decide which ones will fit into a manageable editing process. Depending on your writing and editing experience, you may need fewer steps.

Your Approach to Self-Edits May Look Something Like This

Here are my suggestions on where to start as you learn to edit your own work. There may be parts of this list that you're still not sure about, including exactly how to do developmental edits. I'm going to be breaking down each stage of edits in future books in the series, but you can also dive into the *Before You Hit Send®* course for more information.

1. As you're writing the book, make note of trouble spots. Places where you got stuck, where you struggled to find the right rhythm, where you may have felt the characters weren't cooperating.

2. Finish writing the book.

3. Now, some people like to edit as they go, and that's totally fine. You can adapt this process to work for you if that's your jam! But if you're not making a lot of progress in getting to "The End" because you keep editing and re-editing, well...

then you should finish the book, even just a rough draft, and *then* edit.

4. Let it rest for at least a week.

5. That means don't look at it, don't speak to it, don't open the file. This is hard! But you can be jotting notes for yourself as you're letting it rest. If you have more time, a few weeks is even better. Give yourself some distance. Start writing the next book. Focus on your newsletter, your website, your social media. There are other things you can be doing during this time!

6. After the rest period, read the whole book from start to finish.

7. And / or listen to it (either the parts or the whole).

8. Here you have to figure out what works for you. Giving yourself time to read the whole thing from front to back without long periods of interruption for editing allows you to better see the entire picture of the book and get a sense of the pacing, what's working, what isn't, what's missing and what needs to be further developed. Instead of stopping to edit, take notes on areas you notice need your particular attention.

9. What types of things are you looking for in this read?

- pacing
- story arc
- character arc
- characterization
- relationship development
- mystery / suspense / thriller development
- the beginning
- the end
- world-building
- timeline
- etc.

Basically, you're making sure that all the things that were in your head that need to be on page are on page, and that the story works as a whole unit, and is enjoyable for the reader.

10. *Don't forget to take note of the parts that you really like and think you did well.* You need to work in the high points while you're critiquing your own work, but it's also great to notice what you rock at, so you can do more of it! Plus, some of those parts you mark can become marketing quotes—save yourself time later by pulling things you love now, during edits.

11. Decision time: what part of the story that you took notes on has the most overarching impact on the entire book? Plot? World-building? Rela-

tionship development? Suspense elements? Conflict?

Work on the thing that will have the most overarching impact first. There may be a few big things you're tackling at the same time, such as characterization and relationship development, but don't try to focus on *all* the things all at once. You're honing your writing and editing skills so take them one at a time.

12. Now move on to other developmental edits and edit for those. Keep a checklist that you can run down as you address different things.

13. Time to read the book again from start to finish (yes, really) so you can get the bird's-eye view of the story and all of the changes you've made and new elements you've incorporated.

14. Do any additional developmental edits needed.

15. NOW you can move to line editing. If you haven't already, this is another area of edits where listening can come in handy. Listen to a few chapters to get a sense of your writing style, sentence structure, craft, rhythm, etc.

16. After line edits, you get to move on to the fun, easier things to look for on the copy editing portion of your checklist.

17. Get those dopamine hits in from the quick wins.

18. Now proofread.

19. Then read the book again one last time!

20. And don't forget to celebrate your milestones, accomplishments and work along the way and at "The End"!

I want to reiterate, this is an editing process meant to give you a structured way of breaking down how you look at your work, especially as an early writer. As you begin to publish, this longer process may not always be possible, but the general structure of the stages you work in should be the same.

TAKE ACTION

Using your Editing Checklist Template as a guide, begin outlining the process you're going to use for edits, so you have it to refer to when you're ready to begin editing. This will prevent you from flailing and trying to find your notes from this book and spending time figuring out how to start.

Instead, with your process outlined, you'll be able to get right to it!

Remember, you can and should refine your editing checklist as you learn what *your* books need in editing.

ADDITIONAL RESOURCES

While I was writing this book, I found myself thinking about how to help authors go through edits, especially authors who were going through for one of the first times.

I developed the 5-Pass Editing Method.

There are 4 stages of editing, but the 5-Pass Editing Method breaks the developmental edit stage into two passes. I put this method into a free download that you can access on my website and I've included a bit more detail in Appendix B.

The 5 Passes at a Glance

1. **Big Picture** → Story structure, character arcs, plot
2. **Scene-Level** → Individual scene function and flow
3. **Line Editing** → Sentence clarity, rhythm, voice
4. **Copy Editing** → Consistency, grammar, details
5. **Final Polish** → Formatting, typos, final cleanup

You don't have to do all five passes. Choose what your manuscript needs right now.

CHAPTER 12

HOW LONG SHOULD EDITS TAKE? AKA HOW DO I KNOW WHEN I'M DONE EDITING?

TL;DR

- There's no fixed timeline for editing - it depends on your experience, the book, and the editing stage.
- Editing shouldn't take just a few hours but also shouldn't stretch for months/years.
- Warning signs of over-editing include:
    - Still fiddling with the same manuscript months after typing "The End".
    - Implementing every writing "rule" you discover.
    - No longer loving your story.
    - Fear of completion keeping you from moving forward.
- Use your editing checklist to know when you're done.
- Remember: perfection doesn't exist, but a well-edited book does.

———

Knowing *when* to stop editing can be just as important as where to start. Because if you don't know when to stop, you could be in a situation of overediting—or under-editing and both are detrimental to your story.

Unfortunately for all of us, there's zero percent chance that I can offer an absolute answer to this because the answer depends on so many variables, from the author and their skill and writing experience, to the book and story.

You may realize by now that since everything is subjective, I like to instead offer guidelines so you can apply them to your story and have some idea of when *you* should be done editing.

I suspect that, for an author, sometimes it's difficult to know that happy medium between editing enough and overediting. How do you know? Here's a few things to think about:

- After you've written the book, set it aside for a few weeks and then edit. It will give you some necessary distance from the words and the story, and help you see what's there instead of what's in your head.
- Editing shouldn't take only a few hours, but it also shouldn't take months (or years). If you're still fiddling with the words every day for months after you typed "The End" then it's possible running the risk of overediting.

- Caveat here: if you're only able to work on your book one day a week, yes, it may take months and years, so this isn't meant as a strict timeline guideline, but more of a way of thinking about how long you're holding on to the work rather than moving forward with it.
- If you're researching and implementing every writing rule ever hinted at, you might run the risk of killing your natural voice.

Should you be conscious of your use of certain things like adverbs, dialogue tags, and POV?

Sure.

Should you edit out every "violation" of the "rules" in your manuscript? Probably not.

- On the other hand: be bold, but not too bold. Eschewing punctuation, having random capitalization, and basically not respecting your reader and not considering their experience isn't what I recommend either. Giving your manuscript some polish can enhance the reader experience and, remember, that's our end goal!
- Don't edit so much that you stop loving the story. If you don't love it, why should a reader, or an editor or agent?
- Don't let fear rule you. If you never decide it's ready to send to a publisher, you won't hear "no." But you'll never hear "yes" either. You won't develop that readership you dream of. If you have dreams of making

money, developing a fan base, or hitting a bestseller list, there's no achievement (beyond finishing the book) without the risk of putting your work out there.

- Don't fix every single word just so. If you fiddle with everything, you're going to kill your natural voice, end up overwriting, and probably make the manuscript lifeless and / or stilted.

In truth, the decision to stop editing needs to be part practicality, part intuition, and part courage. There is no magic formula to knowing exactly when the right time to stop editing is, but you need to develop your writing skills and trust in yourself.

Having and following your editing checklist can help with this, especially as you start out. Once you've gone through your personal checklist, it's probably time to stop editing!

I think it's also important to recognize that there's a difference between self-editing for errors, and self-editing in a need for the perfect story. Guess what? Perfection doesn't exist (it doesn't, I promise).

If you're publishing your work, there's always going to be bad reviews, people who hate the book, typos or errors or plot holes people spot. Always. No matter how you're publishing your book (whether trad or indie).

And if you're querying, that "perfect" story is going to go to an editor or agent, and even if it's acquired, they'll more than likely have a whole list of edits that will include rewriting, revising, and deleting those perfect words you worried over for months, and doing it in a way you have no hope of seeing yourself until someone points it out.

Or you're going to publish it, after seven editors have had a look at it, and a reader is going to find that one glaring typo you all missed (I totally had this happen—seven people!).

So at a certain point, let it go. Take a deep breath, cross your fingers, and hit send (or press publish!)

TAKE ACTION

1. Review your current work-in-progress and, being very honest with yourself, assess where you are in the editing process:

- How long have you been editing?
- Are you making meaningful changes or just fiddling?
- Do you still love the story? (It's pretty not uncommon to think you hate your story at certain times, because you've read it so often, but the question is do you still love it or have you overedited it?)

2. Set a reasonable timeline for completing your current round of edits. Consider:

- The type of editing you're doing (developmental, line, etc.).
- Your available time to dedicate to editing.

- Your publishing goals.
- Are you being aspirational in how much you can accomplish and how quickly, or are you basing things around a practical timeline?

3. Using your editing checklist, identify which items you've completed and which still need attention.

4. Focus only on the items appropriate for your current editing stage.

5. If you find yourself stuck in an endless editing loop (you know who you are), try this:

- Write down three specific things you still want to improve about your manuscript.
- Set a deadline to complete these changes.
- After completing them, send the manuscript to a beta reader, critique partner or editor. Or set the date for querying agents/editors. This helps create concrete goals and an endpoint for your editing.

TIPS & TIDBITS

Author Question: What's a reasonable timeline for each stage of edits that I should aim for?

Angela's Response: I knew someone would ask this but I was hoping they wouldn't, lol.

As always, there's a whole lot of "it depends" and "it can vary" involved in this type of answer and for that reason, I don't really know how to give an all-inclusive timeline that's going to work for everyone. It doesn't exist.

Instead, all I have to offer is general advice.

The more experience you get with editing, the less time it's likely to take you BUT the more complicated the world-building, the plot, and the characters, the more time it's going to take you. And short stories go a lot more quickly through edits than 150,000 word fantasy novels.

Developmental edits are going to take the longest. They should take the longest because those are the most impactful, in-depth, and necessary-to-book-success edits you can do. These are the edits that are going to require the most digging in, rewriting and time. Some people can do these edits in weeks, for some it can take months.

This is the stage when you're going to be doing not only the most rewriting, but also the most rereading, in order to ensure that as you changed one thing, you didn't break something else, leave something out, or add something that no longer needs to be added. Rereading is the only way to know that all the pieces fit together.

Probably the one thing I haven't said in this book yet, and that no one often tells you about editing: the best editing comes from not just reading comments and making changes, but from rereading. And rereading again.

Editing isn't just writing and changing, it's a whole lot of reading.

When you move from line edits, to copy edits, to proofreading, each of those stages should take subsequently less time, because in theory there should be less and less changes to make as the book is edited and edited again and again. Plus, in these stages, there's less rereading necessary and more making spot changes.

If you're trying to determine a timeline for edits, my best advice is to give yourself 2–4 months and then double it, especially if it's your first book and you plan on going through each stage of edits and you're determined to spend time creating the best book possible. Everything will take longer than you think.

CHAPTER 13

USING AN AUTHOR STYLE GUIDE AND STORY BIBLE

TL;DR

- Both an author style guide and story bible track details and maintains consistency across your books, saving time during edits.
- Author style guides track things like capitalization preferences, formatting choices, punctuation decisions, spellings.
- Story bibles track things like character descriptions, world-building rules, plot timelines, family trees, setting details.
- There are three types of style guides: standardized (like Chicago Manual of Style), house style guides (publisher-specific), and author style guides (your personal guide).
- Start your author style guide and story bible early—don't wait until you're multiple books into a series.

- Your style guide and story bible help everyone in your editing ecosystem stay on the same page.
- A style guide and a story bible can have minor overlap, but are two different types of documents, tracking two different things.

———

STYLE GUIDES

Along with your editing checklist, another tool that can save you time and energy and should be in your editing arsenal as you build your book backlist is your own style guide.

The author/book/series style guide is a tool most authors skip or don't do, until they're multiple books into a series or backlist. Using a style guide from the start will make your writing life a lot easier down the road. Keywords here: consistency and details.

This style guide can be one that you use for one book, an entire series, or can be an author style guide that houses all of the style you want across your books, whether they're connected or not.

At its core, a style guide tracks details and provides consistency for not only you, but everyone who's editing the books, at any stage of the process.

The details that are tracked in the style guide can vary from guide to guide, and by author, but maintaining a series style guide allows for consistency from book to book, without having to go back to book one when you're writing book five, to see how you spelled a character's name, if you capitalized Vampires, prefer navy or Navy, and use British or North American spelling like gray or grey.

If you're publishing with a traditional publisher, it's worth asking them if a series/book style guide is something they develop, and if you can have a copy of it. If they don't develop one or won't give you a copy, then it's a good idea to create your own.

And sometimes, as one of my beta readers whose books I edit helpfully reminded me, you might work with an indie editor (like me!) who provides a style guide to help get you started or maintains a style guide across the books they've edited for you.

The Different Types of Style Guides

When we talk about style guides in fiction, there are a few things that may be referenced: a **standardized style guide**, a **house style guide**, and the **author's style guide**.

First, **standardized style guides**. For the sake of simplifying this explanation, I'm going to assume people reading this are writing for a North American market. If you're writing for a non-US/non-Canada market, you'll want to research what the regional standardized style may be for that market.

In the US/Canada market, there are three standardized style guides: Chicago Manual of Style (CMoS), Modern Language Association (MLA), and the American Psychological Association (APA). CMoS is the accepted fiction style guide. If you are writing for academia, you'd use the MLA, and if you are writing in the journalistic arena, you'd use APA.

The Chicago Manual of Style (or CMoS) is the style guide that fiction publishers use in North America. This is the basis for most grammar, punctuation, spelling, abbreviations, and other style choices. For example, CMoS is what most publishers will follow to establish their in-house standards across manuscripts for how numbers are handled, how to use quote marks correctly, and how to handle the *'s* after a word that ends in an *s*.

This brings us to the next type of style guide: **house style guides**. While publishers use CMoS as their basis, each publisher has a house style guide they've developed, and many have style guides for individual imprints or lines. In the house style guide, publishers choose how they may depart from CMoS but also establish style rules for individual lines. For instance, a Christian fiction publisher will have their own style guide that details words that aren't allowed to be used in the books or how capitalization of religious terms is handled.

Last, we have the **author's style guide**. This guide gives all of the people in your editing ecosystem— including you—a quick reference from book to book, whether within a series or just within your backlist/frontlist.

One thing to note is that sometimes house style and author's style come into conflict. In times past, house style often overrode author's style, but in current times, publishers are often willing to let author's style prevail, as long as the author:

1. Communicates that they want to use a particular rule, spelling, or capitalization; and
2. Has a reasonable explanation for doing so, especially if it's extremely nonstandard or may appear as an error to the reader.
3. Does not conflict with the publisher's values (again, as an example, going back to the example of a Christian publisher. Their style guide is unlikely to permit the use of something like "goddamn" and this would not be something they would allow despite author style.)

In most cases, publishers will rarely (though it does happen) refuse requests such as this, especially as they become more and more conscious of not homogenizing author voice.

Establishing an author's style guide for yourself is going to make life easier on you in the long run because it saves you time looking up or hunting down details, but it also saves you from having to reject editorial changes every time you go through the editing process, because everyone in the editing process will be on the same page as far as style usage.

I'm going to give you some suggestions for how to develop your author's style guide, as well as templates to help you get started.

What to Include in Your Style Guide

This is not an exhaustive list, but provides you with a starting place. In some cases, your style guide may morph into a more extensive series bible, tracking world-building and character details across a series. Some of what's in a style guide may overlap with a series bible and become even more useful and necessary.

In addition to these specific things, you'll want to make clear in your style guide which dictionary you would like used (most use Merriam-Webster), as well as which standardized style guide you'd like your editor to follow—this is likely going to be Chicago Manual of Style for most of you reading this book.

Names

- Character names (spelling and nicknames) of characters—this is the one thing that should always go in a style guide.
- Pronouns (what pronouns do each of your characters use?
- Names/spelling of real people, celebrities, historical figures, etc.
  - I once read a novel where Rachael Ray's name was misspelled multiple times. No one fact-checked it and added it to the book style guide!
- Places, businesses, towns, street names.
- Brand names and trademarks (make sure you're spelling and capitalizing brands and trademarks correctly).

Capitalization

- Preferred handling of capitalization or not, of words.
  - Examples: CMoS calls for *navy* to only be capitalized in very specific situations, but you may wish to have it capitalized at all times in your military thriller.
- If you're writing sci-fi / fantasy and capitalized words / phrases.
- Setting a preference for capitalization of Black / white when referencing skin color and race.

Italics, bolding, quotes

- Setting up your specific rules for how italics, bolding, or quotation marks may be used in your manuscript.

Non-English words

- If you've included non-English words, do you want them italicized or no? Additional note: the standard here used to be to italicize non-English words in English-language books, but to be more inclusive of non-English words and linguistics, the choice now is often not to italicize. This is something that will be very house style and author style dependent, but my suggestion when you have the option is *not* to italicize, in order to avoid a form of othering (the behavior of emphasizing a difference from the dominant group or culture as "not us" or "less than").

Spelling

- Noted preferences for spelling of words (UK vs. US English, for example, or nonstandard spellings of a word.

Slang, fictional languages, or made-up words

- Noting these can tell a copy editor or proofreader not to "fix" them or query their usage.

Punctuation

- Setting up preferred rules for comma use (Oxford comma, introductory comma after "oh," and other punctuation use that may be nonstandard).

STORY BIBLES

One common source of confusion is the difference between a style guide and a story bible. These are two different documents meant to track two distinct sets of things.

A story bible is a comprehensive reference document that tracks all the story elements, world-building details, character information, and plot points across a book or series. As explained in this chapter, while a style guide focuses on the technical aspects of writing (formatting, spelling preferences, grammar choices, capitalization, name spellings), a story bible contains the actual content and creative elements of your story world, aka your world-building.

In other words:

- Style guides track HOW you write things (spelling, formatting, punctuation choices).
- Story bibles track WHAT you write about (character details, plot, world-building).

Think of it this way:

- A style guide would note that you capitalize "King" when used as a title.
- A story bible would track which characters are Kings, their kingdoms, lineages, and relationships.

Like a style guide, a story bible helps you maintain consistency, but in this case it would include things like:

- Character descriptions/details (ages,

pronouns, gender, hair color, eye color, backgrounds)
- Family trees
- World-building details and rules
- Setting details (for instance, if your small town is a third character, you may need to track details of the town)
- Plot timelines and story arcs
- Magic systems or technology
- Maps and geography
- Historical events in your story world
- Special elements that need tracking across books

While there can be some overlap between style guides and story bibles (both might track character name spelling for instance), they serve two distinct purposes.

If you're writing a series of books, you will likely find you need both - the style guide for consistent presentation and the story bible for consistent content.

TAKE ACTION

1. Download your free Author Style Guide template, found in Appendix D.

2. Start your basic style guide today:

- Download the template.
- Set aside 30 minutes.

- Fill in at least these five essential items:
  1. Character name spellings.
  2. Your preference for Oxford comma.
  3. How you format internal thoughts.
  4. Whether you use US or UK English.
  5. Your chapter heading format.

3. Review your current manuscript:

- Open your work in progress.
- Review the first chapter.
- Note any style decisions you've already made.
- Add these to your style guide.
- Flag any inconsistencies you find for later fixing.

4. Create your "Always Check" list:

- List 3-5 style elements you frequently struggle with.
- Example: "I always mix up afterward/afterwards."
- Add these to a special section in your style guide.
- These become your personal quick-check items during edits.

SECTION THREE
BUILDING TECHNICAL KNOWLEDGE

PREFACE

I dithered around about including this entire section in the book, because a chapter about using word processing programs is obviously so technology-based, and we all know technology changes rapidly, and keeping a book updated with up-to-date information would be a nearly impossible task.

However, over the nearly 2 decades of *Before You Hit Send®*, these lessons have been among the most popular early lessons in creating an efficient and effective editing process, because they teach some very useful and usable information.

With that in mind, I decided to go ahead and include these chapters in the book and ask you to please understand that I know the images and some of the instructions may be out of date. Instead of expecting faithful reproductions of the exact current processes, please look at the core of the information in some cases, not necessarily the specifics.

I also want to emphasize that while Microsoft Word is currently still the most-used software for editing, and what I still recommend (and personally use), there are always improvements being made to other software, such as Google Docs, and there is also the possibility that new programs may be created. Therefore, I reserve the right to say "this is my recommendation at this time and has been for 2 decades" with the understanding that things change rapidly.

Also, like anything, the writing and editing programs you use is a personal, subjective choice and you should use what works most effectively and efficiently for your editing and writing processes.

CHAPTER 14

WHICH WORD PROCESSING PROGRAM TO USE IN EDITS

U sing the right word processing program is like using the correct tool for any job: it will save you time, frustration, and headaches (and you don't need to introduce extra headaches into the editing process)—if you use what works best for you.

But the first thing to know is that probably 90 percent of professional editors you work with are going to use Microsoft Word and they're going to utilize Track Changes and comments for edits.

For that reason (and not because I passionately love Microsoft) my main recommendation for editing is going to be Word. Despite trialing a number of other options over the years, I've found that so far no one has created a word processing program that handles edits quite as smoothly as Word does, and this includes Google Docs.

It's also for this reason that you'll soon come to a few short chapters on how to do edits with Word, since this is mainly what you'd be using when working with an editor.

I want to make it very clear that I'm not saying anyone has to use Word or that there aren't other options, simply that Word is the option that is best equipped to handle the demands of an editing process, and that the expectation will be to use Word when working with a traditional publisher, as well as many professional editors and agents.

Microsoft Word

This is the most common word processing program used in edits, with the ability to use Track Changes, document comments from multiple reviewers, view the document with and without changes, compare documents, merge documents, and customize how the changes appear.

Scrivener

While you may choose to write in Scrivener, and many authors do, it's not a great program for doing edits, and has a pretty distinct lack of function in this area. It's just really not what it's meant for. My recommendation here is to write in Scrivener but then export the document at the editing stage (and don't try to put it back in Scrivener and out again, because you're going to spend more time making sure your formatting isn't jacked than you want to).

Pages

The Apple Mac answer to MS Word, it's an alternative and you can use it (I have certainly tried), but the editing features aren't as robust or easy to use as you may wish, and it always seems to have considerable lag time.

Google Docs

For a long while, Google Docs didn't have any editing capabilities. While they've slowly added some function-ality, and it has the advantage of more than one person being able to work in a document at the same time, in real time, it's also limited and may be difficult for use with multiple people.

Of concern is that in 2024, there were also claims that Google had shut down one or more author's access to their account and documents, based on the material in their shared documents (more explicit romances shared with beta readers).

As of the time of writing this, Google Docs also can't handle large numbers of comments/suggestions, and becomes increasingly laggy and buggy the more editing that's done.

In order to give Google Docs a fair try once again before I published this book, I used it for the beta reading process. What I found was that I still needed to export the documents from Google to Word, in order to merge and compare documents, and it created a headache of extra work and time. I won't be doing that again!

Last, Microsoft Word's .docx format still seems to be the preferred format for inputting into formatting software (weirdly to me, because Word inputs so much hidden formatting into documents), so it still seems a more straightforward path to work within Word.

For all these reasons, I am not currently recommending Google Docs for shared editing.

Other Options

There are certainly other options to explore such as WPS OfficeFree, LibreOffice, Atticus and others, if you continue to search for an alternative.

TAKE ACTION

If you don't already have Microsoft Word, consider getting it now so you can get comfortable with it before you are deep diving into edits. (Tip: there are legitimate places to get the Microsoft Suite at a deep discount. If you want some suggestions, email me and I will point you toward them.)

CHAPTER 15

EDITING WITH MICROSOFT WORD —TRACK CHANGES

To build up your editing skills from scratch, it's important to spend a few short chapters setting you up for success with a foundation in how to edit with Microsoft Word. This is the word processing program most frequently used by professional editors, so chances are you're going to be using it throughout your author career.

Even if you use Word already and are semi-familiar with it, you may find I have a few tricks for you to hone your use of the Review features.

If you're not already familiar with them, Track Changes and Find/Replace are two Word tools that you should consider your new best friends and become intimately familiar with. I suggest that any time you're engaged in edits (especially in later rounds), whether for yourself or your publisher, or with critique partners, **Track Changes should be on**, so both you and your editor can see:

1. what's been changed; and
2. any errors you've inserted with the changes.

It's quite common for errors to be inserted during the editing process, because of accidental keystrokes, accidentally starting to type in this document instead of an email, etc., so it's best to be prepared for how you're going to spot those accidental insertions (you never know when a foster kitten is going to run across your keyboard!).

You should also always expect that any time you make changes to a document, you're also inserting errors. Worst-case-scenario thinking like this will help make you more cautious and more alert. Plus, it's something editors know is true: errors are inserted at every stage of edits.

But, as authors, you may want to track changes for another reason not having to do with errors at all. Tracking changes also allows you to have a visual record of editorial changes you've made, like where you've added a new character detail, changed a plot element, or deleted a section of dialogue.

This is important not just for remembering when you've changed something that might affect later scenes or details, but also important in case you want to *reverse the change.* Also, for what it's worth, it can help to prove version history should you ever be engaged in a copyright dispute.

How to Track Changes in Word

Word has a robust review feature with a number of options, and in this chapter we're focusing on Track Changes. If you're not already, you should also become familiar with the Comment feature, as well as the different ways of viewing changes and comments (inline or in balloons).

I've seen some editors and authors type comments directly into the text, rather than using the commenting feature. *This is something to avoid,* because I've then also seen those same editors and authors accidentally incorporate the editorial comment into the text (in fact, I saw this in a published book I read recently).

NO HEADACHES LATER

Using the Comment feature allows you to pinpoint/highlight the exact words, sentence, or section you're directing your comment to, and it will never accidentally become part of the text!

In the resource list we provide, I've linked to an article that illustrates beautifully why use of Track Changes and Comments is imperative at a certain stage and why inserting editorial comments into text is a BAD IDEA. This also goes for highlighting, which is *not* a substitute for Track Changes. I use highlighting rarely, usually to indicate repetition, but I try to avoid it because it's easy to lose highlighted text in the manuscript, and to forget to take it out before sending the file to the copy editor. Highlighting can also become stubbornly stuck in the formatting and end up sneaking its way into published work (something I've also observed).

Here's what it looks like to turn Track Changes on in Word. I'm using Word 365 so your version of Word may look slightly different.

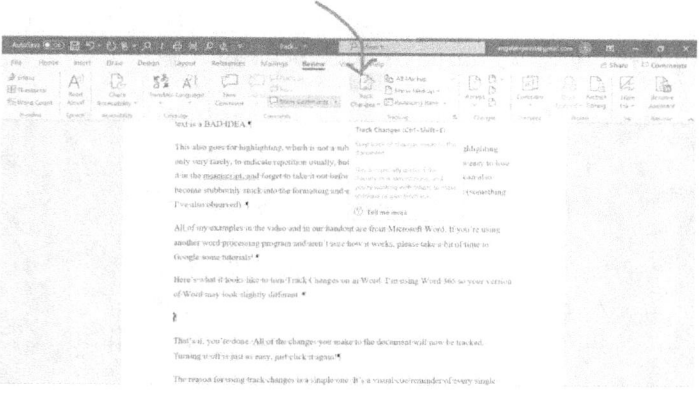

That's it, once you click it and it's highlighted, you're done. All of the changes you make to the document will now be tracked. Turning it off is just as easy; just click it again!

The reason for using Track Changes is a simple one. It's a visual cue/reminder of every single change that's made to your manuscript, whether insertion or deletion.

Once you've made your changes, the Review toolbar makes it easy to go from one change to the next.

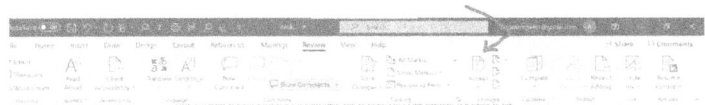

The danger of using Track Changes and the "next" function is that it can become tempting, especially in edits with your editor, to look only at the changes and not the rest of the text. Sometimes this is fine, but especially in the beginning stages of edits, you want to read the whole scene, chapter, or even book in order to find other things that might need changing as well.

It can make edits more difficult for your editing partner, and make your own edits less robust, if they spend literally hours on the developmental and line edits they send you, only to have you return them within the space of an hour or a day because you've only focused your attention on the specific things they pointed out, not on the overall document.

Don't depend so heavily on that "next" function that you don't spend time going through the manuscript yourself!

TAKE ACTION

Take 15 minutes to explore Word's Review features:

- Turn on Track Changes and practice making edits.
- Add a comment.

- Try viewing the document in different modes (Original, Show Markup, Simple Markup).
- Experiment with showing markup from specific reviewers, viewing markup in the sidebar, and understanding how certain views hide markup (but don't delete markup from your document, so be aware of that!).

TIPS & TIDBITS

Author Question: If you turn off Track Changes, do all previous edits go away or "get accepted?"

Angela's Response: No. You have to physically select to accept the changes. Turning it on and off doesn't affect previously tracked changes.

Author Question: At what stage do you suggest turning on Track Changes, even during the first pass of heavier edits? I love Track Changes but sometimes it drives me batty when the manuscript is rainbow colors. Do you accept in batches, say per round of revisions? Or just read in "Final"?

Angela's Response: I don't usually have a hard and fast rule about when to start using Track Changes because I think it really varies from person to person. Use it when it makes sense for you to do so.

CHAPTER 16

EDITING WITH MICROSOFT WORD— FIND AND REPLACE

I f you're not very familiar with Microsoft Word, or are afraid of the Find and Replace function, I'm going to show you something magical in this lesson. No burying the lede here!

Find and Replace has a variety of uses, from basic polishing (finding double spaces, etc.) to word replacement, to searching and destroying adverbs, to getting rid of punctuation, and to helping with later steps in the editing process (finding garbage/filter words, for example).

The Dark Side!

But there is a dark side to Find and Replace: if you don't use it correctly, you will be using it to *introduce errors into your manuscript* without even realizing it!

Here's how to use this tool correctly:

1. **Turn Track Changes on.** If you're going to do a Find and Replace, you'll need Track Changes on. We already discussed that you'll want to work with them on when you're editing anyway, but just in case, turn them on now. This will let you see the replacements Word has made and ensure you don't make any errors.

2. **Open Find or Find and Replace.** This tool is located in different places in different versions of Word. Because it's something you may frequently use, you may want to put it in your Quick Access Toolbar.

3. You can also use the key combination Ctrl+F (or Cmd+F on a Mac) and it will open Find on the sidebar. Ctrl+H will open Find and Replace (on a Mac, go to the Edit menu, click on Find and select Advanced Find and Replace to access the full range of options).

Find Whole Words Only

There are going to be times when you'll just want to Find words, and times when you want to Find and Replace. There's an important box for you to be aware of in both instances, but especially in Find and Replace: the *Find whole words only* checkbox.

To locate this, look under Find and Replace and then **Advanced Options**.

The *Find whole words only* checkbox is important because if you do a find for "the" for instance, it's also going to find every instance of "their," "lathe," "thermostat," and any other word that contains the letter combinations of "the". By checking *Find whole words only* you will see only "the" as it stands alone.

Let's say you're doing a Find and Replace, and you *don't* check *Find whole words only*, this can have disastrous results.

For example, let's take this paragraph, which is a quirky sample paragraph I wrote when I created the course back in 2009. It's meant to be silly and not great, and you'll also see it used as an example in future books:

Jack couldn't stop thinking about her. Night and day, he was consumed by thoughts of her, thoughts that made him crazy, overwhelmed all thoughts of anything else and drove him to a frenzy. This needed to stop, he had to work her out of his system, stop this obsession with her and move on. He had work to do, a major business deal to work on. She was just a woman, like any other woman, why couldn't he stop thinking of her? Jacking off in the shower hadn't helped, had barely taken the edge off! Walking down the street, images of her played through his head.

I'll be using this paragraph as an example of many of the things we'll be editing for, so it's purposely riddled with errors (in case you were wondering if Angela really isn't so bright after all!).

To start with, I've decided that I don't like the hero's name. I want to change it to Horatio. Horatio's a nice name, don't you think? So let's go ahead and change Jack to Horatio.

I'm going to do a Find and Replace:

Find what: Jack
Replace with: Horatio

Here's what that gives us:

> Horatio couldn't stop thinking about her. Night and day, he was consumed by thoughts of her, thoughts that made him crazy, over-whelmed all thoughts of anything else and drove him to a frenzy. This needed to stop, he had to work her out of his system, stop this obsession with her and move on. He had work to do, a major business deal to work on. She was just a woman, like any other woman, why couldn't he stop thinking of her? Horatioing off in the shower hadn't helped, had barely taken the edge off! Walking down the street, images of her played through his head.

Hmm! Do you see the problem we've introduced into the manuscript?

> Horatioing off in the shower hadn't helped, had barely taken the edge off!

We forgot a step: the box for *Find whole words only* wasn't checked. Checking that box lets Word know to look for only whole words, not partial words!

So, that's the basic functionality of Find and Replace. An author, Susanna Fraser, who participated in a past workshop I ran, shared her experience with the dangers of not using the *Find whole words only* option when using Find and Replace. I love this real-world example and asked if I could share it in future workshops, to emphasize the importance of using it carefully:

 I never knew about the whole words option, and I had to deal with almost the exact issue you use in your example! The hero of *The Sergeant's Lady* was originally named Jack, and when I decided to change his name to Will, I did a global Find and Replace...only to discover on my next read through that suddenly my army characters were wearing uniform *willets*. Oops.

What About Possessives and Past Tense?

If you use *Find whole words only* in Find and Replace, will that take care of finding and replacing for every form of a word? For example, if you use an *'s* or an *-ed* in a word, will it replace those words?

Let's talk through this:

Say you want to do a Find and Replace of "Jane" with "Horatio" and you have a sentence that says:

Jane's mood was ugly. Jane was an angry, angry girl.

Now we do the following Find and Replace with *Find whole words only* checked:

Find what: Jane
Replace with: Horatio

This gives the following result:

Horatio's mood was ugly. Horatio was an angry, angry girl.

So, even when you check *Find whole words only*, Word still recognizes words with an *'s* as needing to be replaced, because it considers the whole word, the apostrophe, and the *s* as three separate elements of the word.

To see what I mean, try finding the possessive apostrophe and replacing it with a comma, then try finding the *s* and replacing it with a *d*. You'll see the way that Word treats elements of text separately so they can be found and replaced separately.

This means that if you do a Find and Replace for a word that also has a version that ends in *ed* (like "happen" and "happened"), *Find whole words only* will mean that Word changes every instance of "happen," but *not* "happened," because that is a whole word all on its own.

What Else Can We Use Find and Replace For?

An editor in a course I taught once asked, "I can't think of a time when an editor would need to use this feature, am I correct?"

No, that's wrong!

There's a reason I've spent several pages talking about Find and Replace: I use it *all the time* to find standard errors, especially in punctuation. I use Find and Replace to get rid of double spaces, double periods, space+periods, to convert double hyphens to em dashes, en dashes to em dashes, and so much more! When I edit a very new author, I actually use this to see if we need to do a fix for lack of contractions in dialogue (I'll talk about this in a later book on Developmental Editing). This tool is every bit as valuable for editors as it is for authors.

And how do you replace double spaces with single spaces? It's as simple as hitting the space bar twice in the search field, and once in the replace field. Then run it again until Word tells you it made 0 replacements.

TAKE ACTION

- Create a test document (just duplicate your work in progress and name it clearly) and practice using Track Changes with these exercises:
  - Change a character's name
  - Change double space to single space

- Change exclamation point to a period ("!" to ".")
- Find and delete "slowly"
- Add comments
- Accept/reject changes
- View the document in different markup modes.
- Practice using Find Whole Words Only by searching for is, said, laughed, and he's.

CHAPTER 17

EDITING WITH MICROSOFT WORD —CUSTOMIZING THE QUICK ACCESS TOOLBAR

TL;DR

- The Quick Access Toolbar is a customizable bar in Microsoft Word that gives you one-click access to your most frequently used editing tools.
- Adding editing functions like Find, Replace, and Track Changes to your Quick Access Toolbar can save significant time during edits.
- Taking a few minutes to set up your Quick Access Toolbar now will make your editing process more efficient for every manuscript going forward.

———

This may seem like an odd chapter to include, but one of the important things about learning a good editing process that you can *repeat* is finding ways to take shortcuts and save time, that don't negatively impact the book or reading experience.

That's why I love Word's Quick Access Toolbar. This toolbar lives across the top of your Word screen and can be customized to provide—you guessed it—quick access to different Word functions you may use.

Here's a screenshot of what mine looked like a few years ago. The Quick Access Toolbar is the part that's at the bottom of the image.

You can see that I have a few functions on mine: Find, Replace, Breaks, Search, Italics. I've added the things I use most frequently so I can quickly access them (I'm not a person who uses keystroke commands so the Quick Access Toolbar serves a great function for me).

You can add a variety of functions based on your most frequent uses, and you can also change whether the Quick Access Toolbar appears above the main toolbar/ribbon or below it.

Take a look at Microsoft's instructions for adding to the Quick Access toolbar and add Find and Replace to it, along with anything else, such as Next Change/Comment, that you might use in editing and writing. Just don't overwhelm your toolbar, start small so you get used to using it.

TAKE ACTION

Set up your Quick Access Toolbar with a few of my favorites:

- Track Changes
- New comment
- Find
- Replace
- Style
- Breaks

CHAPTER 18

BACKING UP YOUR WORK

TL;DR

- Back up your work DAILY. This isn't optional —it's a crucial part of being a professional writer.
- Use multiple backup methods rather than relying on a single solution. Cloud storage + local backup gives you redundancy.
- Your backup system should be as automated as possible to ensure it actually gets done.
- Create and stick to a consistent file naming convention that helps you quickly identify versions and status of manuscripts.

———

Hopefully, I'm preaching to the choir on this one, and each and every one of you has a fantastic backup system in place for saving your work daily.

Sadly, it seems like every day I hear of people who aren't using a regular backup system and have catastrophic failures and loss of information, work, and files. And, let's be honest, even backups can fail, so having a system in place that provides multiple backups is never a bad idea!

But, just in case you don't already have a system in place, I think backing up is one of the most important basic parts of the editing and writing process and one that we can't ignore. I'd feel remiss if I didn't do my part to make sure you're backing up your work. I never want to hear of any author losing their work!

Back. Up. Your. Work. All of it! (And your pictures too!)

Backup Options

There are so many options now for people to back up their work, both free and paid, to a device or in the cloud, that there is NO reason you aren't backing up daily. If you aren't backing up and you lose your work at some point, well, that's a painful lesson you really wouldn't have had to learn! None of this "it won't happen to me" mentality allowed. That's magical thinking. It can and probably will happen to you, if it hasn't already. Save yourself a lot of recriminations and tears and back that work up!

Let's talk options (before we do this, please note these options change so frequently, it's difficult to keep up, so there may be changes in the below):

All of these options have both a free plan and a paid plan:

1. Dropbox
2. Aomei Backupper Standard
3. iDrive
4. Perfect Backup
5. Microsoft OneDrive
6. Google Drive
7. Email. Some authors like to email copies of their work to an alternate email account, using a Gmail or other account dedicated *only* to storing email copies they've emailed themselves of work in progress.

I do *not* suggest/support either burning to CDs (most of you probably don't even have a computer that does that anymore, lol) or saving to a flash drive as a secure form of backup because both forms are easily damaged and corrupted, and therefore the information isn't as securely backed up as could be.

The advantage of some of the different sites in the list above is that once you set one of these up initially, there's not a lot you need to remember to do. For instance, Dropbox, iDrive, Perfect Backup, and programs like those run in the background, updating automatically. As long as you've set up your main work folders to be part of Dropbox, whenever you save your work to those folders it will be backed up automatically in the cloud. It's nice to have a method that you don't have to think about or remember to do, especially if you're not great about keeping on top of things like this. And if this is the case for you, choose something as automated as possible so you're always backed up!

Personally, I've used (and use) several methods. Currently I use Dropbox as well as Google Drive.

You may also want to do a deeper dive into true backups versus syncing, in order to understand your options there as well!

Using Dropbox or Google Drive from an author's perspective

I love Dropbox, but having a backup isn't even the biggest reason I love it. I write primarily on my MacBook, but also on a PC desktop, my iPod Touch and now my iPad, too. Before I got Dropbox, I'd have to email my book to myself, then download it to whichever computer I was going to use, then save it and email it to myself when I was going to move to a different one. More often than not, I'd find myself working on the wrong computer so then I'd have to merge the older version I'd worked on with the newer version I'd emailed over (or forgotten to email over).

Now the most current version just automagically appears where I need it. AND it's a backup. Love it!

—Shannon Stacey, Author

I would say similar things about Google Drive, which I use to run my business (calendar, worksheets, Meet, email, desktop integration, file sharing—love it!)

—Helen Conway, Translator

...And an Editor's!

I will also tell you that I had an opportunity to (unfortunately) practice what I preach years ago. I experienced a fatal hard drive failure and had to have the hard drive replaced on my Mac. Had I not been using Carbonite, which I no longer use, and Dropbox at that time, I would have lost everything on my computer and not had access to important work files, on Dropbox, during the period when the hard drive was being replaced.

Don't ever, ever assume hard drive failure and data loss won't happen to you. Back up your work. It's like having a will and life insurance—we all need them because, well, eventually we'll all need them.

Do your research to decide what the best option(s) are for you, but do make sure you have a plan in place!

One More Tip: Use a File Naming Convention

I encourage all authors to adopt a file naming convention now, not later, so that your backups make sense if you need to return to them.

A file naming convention also helps your editor locate your work: I can't tell you how insane it drives me to get submissions where the documents are named "manuscript," "synopsis," "book." Imagine how many thousands of these files exist—how are we to tell them apart?

When I work on edits with an author, I use a combination of file name, initials, and version number. For files for myself, I use file name and version number.

For example:

BookTitle_Edits_AJ_V1
BookTitle_Edits_CB_V2

For myself I use this convention:

DescriptiveDocumentName_V5

You'll thank yourself for using a file convention— starting *now*!

TAKE ACTION

If you're not already using a *daily* backup method, choose one and set it up this weekend.

This.

Weekend.

To do: **Organize *daily* backups!**

SECTION FOUR
BUILDING YOUR EDITING RELATIONSHIPS

CHAPTER 19

EDITOR-AUTHOR (AND OTHER TEAM MEMBERS) RELATIONSHIP(S)

L isten, the editor-author relationship shouldn't be adversarial! But like any relationship, it takes work, good communication, and a willingness to adapt.

TL;DR

A few key things to remember:

- Not every editor is your perfect match, and that's okay! Just like dating, you might need to try a few before finding the right one.
- Your editor should respect your voice while helping polish your story. And you should be open to feedback while protecting your vision.
- Check your ego at the door (both of you!) because ego is the biggest barrier to creating an awesome book.
- You, the author, have final say on changes—

but give those editorial suggestions fair consideration before saying no.
- Be professional! Meet deadlines, communicate clearly, and remember that a simple "thank you" goes a long way.
- The goal is creating the best possible reading experience, and that happens when authors and editors work as a team.
- Communicating with your team members can create a support system that works both for you and with you. Don't try to go it alone.

———

Over the years, I've heard from many authors who struggle or have struggled with their relationship with an editor. And since I've worked with thousands of authors, I can guarantee there have been a few authors who struggled with their relationship with me.

Why? Because the editor-author relationship isn't always one that's guaranteed to be compatible, just like any other relationship. And like any other relationship, it's one that takes work, good communication, and a willingness to adapt.

So I thought I would write out some thoughts about the editor-author relationship and what it might look like, how it may—or may not—work, and what expectations everyone should come into the relationship with.

This should be helpful to everyone but perhaps especially those who've never worked with an editor, and don't have an idea of what an editorial relationship can/should look like.

A delicate balance of critique and compliments

One of the strongest points I want to make is that the editorial relationship isn't meant to be an adversarial one.

Let me take you on a journey to circle back around to this point, now that I've led with it.

While you're reading this book or taking *Before You Hit Send®*, or in my world via my newsletter, a membership or a workshop, maybe you'll find me a little blunt in some of the things I say or the comments I make.

The straightforward approach is one of my personality traits as both a person and an editor, and so you may find that I deliver things directly, sometimes bluntly, and occasionally with the "no bullshit" approach (while still trying to take an empathetic and kind approach because I'm not here to hurt anyone's feelings and disguise blunt as "mean" or "rude").

Not only do I favor a straightforward approach, but one of my goals for authors who take *Before You Hit Send®*, and who are reading this book, is getting you used to facing critique, both your own *and from other people*.

I've found that for an author, getting blunt feedback can be a *lot* harder to accept in an editorial relationship than it can be even from beta readers or critique partners.

There's something about seeing editors as a sort of "final authority" that makes so many authors have an almost unconscious wish to turn in a manuscript for edits and receive accolades and praise from their editor and be told "no edits needed", as a sign that they've "nailed it".

This is despite the fact that the editorial process is one that's *intended* specifically to give/receive critique (edits) alongside the praise, and that edits are desirable to help make the book an even stronger reading experience.

Yet, for some reason, some authors often seem to silently hope that the manuscript will come back with "job well done, no edits needed!" rather than hoping the editor will dig in and give insightful critique.

And if that critique comes with more honesty, or bluntness, it can just feel painful to many authors, rather than helpful, perhaps because that hidden wish for a gold star from the editor makes it difficult to process the feedback as anything but negative.

Maybe for that reason, knowing the heart of hearts of authors, it's also incredibly difficult as an editor (at least in my personal experience) to *give* blunt feedback, because I want the author to understand I appreciate and respect the hard work and talent that's gone into a book, and I'm not trying to crush anyone's dreams, make anyone cry, or give them a dread of the editing experience, but I also want to be thorough in the critique and polishing of the book.

So giving honest feedback and critique is a delicate balancing act of exact phrasing, avoiding emotionally loaded words, and offering genuine praise and compliments.

As an editor, I spend literal hours crafting the edit letter with careful phrasing, and making sure the comments within the manuscript balance the right tone. That "how to phrase this" part of editing is a time-consuming part of the process simply because I want the author to not get hung up on tone, but instead focus on the content of the edits.

I think many professional editors feel similarly to me. We want you to get as much out of our editorial brains as possible, but whew, sometimes it's hard to straight-up say when something isn't working, without trying to couch it in polite phrasing that hopefully won't sting as much. Our goal is to give enough infor-mation for you to understand *why* something may not be working.

It's a fine line of "just the right amount of honesty but not too much honesty" that editors may have to walk. It's also true that because authors are individuals, some authors are more sensitive to edits than others, so we have to learn the needs of our individual clients and deliver our feedback in a way best suited to each individ-ual. That's one reason finding an editor who's a good fit for you while being good at giving feedback is so critical.

Ego

I also like to remind authors—and editors—that the *one biggest obstacle* to good editing is ego. Ego on *both* sides of the editing relationship. If everyone enters into the editorial process thinking there's no room for change, growth, or learning, and thinking they're infallible or always right, then the editorial process will fail, because ego has created a roadblock to delivering the best possible reader experience.

Whether you're an author or editor, taking your ego out of the process, being able to admit you're not always right, or things don't always have to be done your way will put you in a better position to develop an excellent working relationship with your editor or the authors you're editing.

The working relationship has to work for *you*

In some way you've chosen this editor you're working with, whether you hired them or contracted with the publisher who hired them. Sure, maybe you didn't get to handpick them in the latter case, but you trusted the press enough to give them your book and, in return, give you a qualified editor.

If you don't trust the press is going to give you a qualified, professional editor, don't sign a contract with them!

If you're the one doing the choosing, don't just choose the editor with the lowest price or the flashiest website or even the biggest reputation. Research, talk to your fellow authors, talk to prospective editors, figure out what you're looking for in an editor (make a list), and find one who is going to give you what you most need for that particular book.

Your editor isn't (shouldn't be) there to rewrite your voice, but should be there to work with you to polish, trim, critique, cut, and sometimes be ruthless in places you can't because you're too close to the work.

If you have an editor who's rewriting your work, this could be the sign of a problem with the editorial boundaries. If you're an editor with an author who expects you to rewrite their work, this could be the sign of a problem with the editorial boundaries.

It works both ways: understanding the expectations and boundaries of the editor and the author roles in this partnership.

Real Talk

The other part of the editor/author working relationship is acting with professionalism. Things like deadlines, calm, and kind communication all make a difference in how you build an excellent working relationship with your publishing team.

First, let's talk about deadlines, because this may be one of the trickiest parts of being an author, whether you're working with an indie editor or a traditional publisher. No matter how you're publishing, you are going to end up trying to figure out how long it's going to take you to write the book and deliver it for edits, to kick off the publishing process.

If I give you any advice you take, I hope this is one of those things: overestimate how long it will take you, don't underestimate (or in other words, be practical, not aspirational in your writing goals).

No exaggeration, your entire publishing timeline is going to depend on your ability to get the delivery deadlines as close to accurate as possible, so when someone asks you "when can you deliver that?" *give yourself space*.

Because once you miss your first deadline, or someone misses their deadline *to you*, all of the timeline behind that has to be shortened or moved back.

For indie editors, this may impact their ability to schedule other clients, how much time they can spend with your book, or other tasks in their small business and/or personal life (especially if you need them to perform edits in a shortened time period).

And let's not forget: this is also true for indie authors whose editors miss their deadlines! Indie authors also have a schedule and personal lives that are interrupted by missed deadlines.

If you're working with traditional publishers, meeting deadlines for both manuscripts and edits is a cornerstone of the entire publishing, marketing and selling process.

When editors can't guarantee to the other departments that the author will deliver on time, it's very difficult for the editor to convince everyone at the publisher—from retail to marketing to social media to everyone in leadership—that it's a good idea to take a chance on special opportunities, more marketing money, and even sell-in to retailers (aka when the sales team convinces a brick and mortar store to carry the book, and in what quantities).

Just meeting deadlines makes you a more predictable author to work with, which makes everyone happy, but more importantly, makes them trust that they can depend on you.

Having said all that about deadlines, I do want to

make it extra, extra clear that *no editor* wants you to burn yourself out, put your health (physical or mental) at risk, or neglect your personal life in order to meet deadlines.

All of us do understand that life happens, things happen. Just like we want you to be kind to us, we also want to be kind to you, and we will extend you help, and usually even extra time, if you tell us you need it.

BUT! We would just rather know as soon as possible if you're not going to be able to meet the deadline, because that allows us to rearrange as needed.

The worst thing you can do is to ghost your editor or not alert them when you're struggling, and instead let them think (even by virtue of being silent about your struggles) that the manuscript is going to be delivered by the deadline.

Editors are on your team and can be your greatest publishing ally (whether indie or traditional publishing)! We want to help you have the best publishing experience possible, but that means you need to communicate with your editor and publishing team and let us know so we can help you.

Please don't try to just struggle through or go it alone. Be honest with your team and work with them to make a plan that's going to work for you (and for everyone else!).

And once again, I want to state for the record, though I'm talking directly to authors in this book/chapter, the reverse also holds true. The standards apply to everyone in this system, not just the author! So if you're an editor, copy editor, proofreader, beta reader, etc., this chapter is just as relevant for you.

When we're talking about professionalism, at the risk of sounding overly preachy, and perhaps stating the obvious, everything also works more smoothly if you conduct yourself kindly and calmly in emails or interactions with any team member you work with.

Publishing is a small world, both inside a publisher and across the larger publishing ecosystem, and acts of arrogance, rudeness and negativity do get shared when they *become a hallmark* of an author's interactions (listen, you're human and allowed to be, we're talking about a pattern, not a one-off).

Or, as another example, if someone on the publishing team sees the author kvetching on social media about, say, hating the cover, rather than taking their feedback to the cover art department, or directly to the cover artist (if you've been working directly with one), and asking if there's anything that can be done. This is something that can burn bridges with individual team members, with your publisher and with others in the publishing industry who are paying attention.

Last, and this might seem obvious but it bears repeating: saying thank you never hurts. There are a lot of people who work on a book, even indirectly just getting it to the reader, and *all* of the team members remember when there's an author who's sent an email to be forwarded to the team saying *thank you*. And if you're working with individuals you hired yourself, thank you is always welcome if you've appreciated their work.

Find a good mindset to receive edits

When we're talking about the editor-author relationship, I think this is important to remember and might surprise some of you that it's an editor saying it…

Your editor is absolutely *not* always right (oh sure, we like to think we are, but we're not) and you should absolutely ask questions and say no to edits and suggested changes if they don't feel right to you.

Remembering that editors (and other people in the publishing ecosystem you work with) aren't always right can help lessen some of the resentment you may feel toward edits, but also allow you to realize that there are times they are right, as well.

It creates a situation where you become more comfortable having a dialogue about edits, rather than feeling as if you're obligated to say yes to every editorial request.

That said, before you say "no" during the course of looking at edits, just be sure you've actually given yourself time and distance from the edits, so you have an opportunity to give them fair thought, and you've given the critique/comments/feedback a chance.

I've worked one-to-one with thousands of authors through my multi-faceted publishing career and here's a fact: *no two authors approach getting edits the same.*

Some authors hate edits and will find a way to argue every edit, convinced that the editor simply doesn't understand their voice, their vision, their story. Some authors want to say they've been edited but won't make any edits. They just want to be able to say they had an editor. Some authors absolutely love being edited and dive into it wholeheartedly as an opportunity to make the book better. Some authors don't understand that *they* are the final authority on the book, and because they think every suggestion and change has to be accepted, they come to dread edits. And some authors fall on the spectrum somewhere in the midst of a few of these descriptions.

The mindset with which you approach edits can impact your relationship with your editor, yes, but perhaps even more important, it can impact your relationship with your book and impact the reader's experience.

If your mindset is one of dread or loathing of edits, that can certainly create an adversarial relationship with your editor, even inadvertently, and close you off to the potential of creating an even better reading experience. The editor isn't always right, but neither is the author!

An editor should also approach an author's return comments with an open mind. We're human too. Sometimes it will be hard, especially when we feel strongly about a suggested change or edit. But again, as I said above, this is your book, not ours, and so you're the final authority on changes.

A fun aside: we (developmental editors) hate copy edits as much as you do because someone is pointing out all the stuff we missed and making it look like maybe we didn't do our job (we did, copy editing isn't something the developmental editor should be focusing on). Then we remember how thankful we are for the copy editor because they make us (editor and author) look good.

Remember those "rules" don't really exist. Until they do.

There are going be some editors who tell you a rule is absolute (e.g., you must use one POV per chapter, you can't ever use an adverb, and you should delete every single dialogue tag).

If an editor insists there's a writing "rule"…*they're wrong*.

No, you can't tell them I said so (oh, fine, go ahead, tell them I said so).

But, again, an editorial relationship isn't meant to be an adversarial one, so approach how you disagree with this moderately. Still, I can't emphasize this enough: no one has been appointed King or Queen of Writing Rules (not even me, sadly, because I do like sparkly tiaras) and no one can tell you *absolutely* about most things (see how I avoided the absolute there? lol!). But truly, even some punctuation and grammar rules have multiple schools of thought, because of voice, language, style, region and more.

And I will say this as well again: the editor isn't always right and you, the author, have full authority over your book, over saying no, over the changes you acquiesce to.

Yes, even when you're writing for a traditional publisher.

But. Oh, big but here, keep in mind that publishers do have what's called "house style" and often will expect to copy edit and proofread your book within that style. This is usually not the time to choose the Oxford comma or use of semi-colons as the hill you want to die on when working with your publisher.

However, when we're talking about your voice, style that may feel othering (such as putting non-English words in italics), or a general overall style that has a strong impact on how the reader experiences your story, such as how E.E. Cummings (yes, I did capitalize that correctly based on his preference!) used mixed lowercase and uppercase for effect, then it is worth starting a conversation with your editor. Those are important reasons to push back against "house style" and initiate a conversation with your editor about suggested changes.

Kill Your Darlings (Ugh!)

This is such a loaded phrase. *I don't love it.* You might not love it. But many of you will recognize what it means so I'm going to use it.

In the course of your writing career, there are going to be times when an editor is going to ask you to "kill your darlings", aka delete a favorite word, phrase, sentence or even scene. (Note: One of my editing clients beta read this book and inserted the comment "or a character" here, and that is true. I did that, lol.)

Your editor will most likely ask without knowing it's something you're particularly fond of, and you're not going to want to get rid of it. But after some thought, you're going to. And it might not be that day, that week, or that year, but eventually you'll realize they were right. It's okay if you never tell them, though (probably, they already know). If you want to tell them, gifts of chocolate, alcohol, and crafted goods are always welcome.

Alternately, you may change it and then forever regret it because they were wrongity wrong wrong wrong. That could happen too.

Or perhaps, at some point, your editor will gracefully (or not-so-gracefully) concede on a suggested change, something you disagree with, and you will choose not to make the change.

Later, readers will point out that thing as something they hated, didn't understand, wished you'd expanded, or should have done differently. You don't ever need to admit *this* to your editor either. But we'll still know.

On the other hand, at some other time, your editor will gracefully (or not-so-gracefully) concede on a suggested change, something you disagree with, and you will choose not to make the change.

Later, readers will point out that thing you chose not to change as something they loved, thought was a great piece of writing, adored as a detail. The thing the editor wanted you to cut was the thing that the reader will bring attention to as amazing. You will be totally vindicated.

Try not to rub it in. Too much.

The idea here is, there will be times when you will each need to understand the other person's point of view. But notice in the end, the control and the choice is always the author's. You get to choose, you have final say, because it's your book. Your name on the cover.

Not every author and editor are a good match

Oooh boy, maybe this should have been the first point I made, because it's a critical thing to remember.

You aren't going to vibe with every editor.

Maybe not even the editor your critique partner loves. Maybe not even me. It's okay! It's like matching readers to books, not all are meant to be partnered together.

Every editor isn't a good match for every author. Or for every book. Or genre. Or every stage of edits.

You need the right editor for you, who's going to vibe with your book, has experience with your genre, and specializes in the stage of edits you're in (so don't hire a developmental editor for proofreading and vice versa, they're two different skillsets).

You also don't need to be friends with your editor.

In fact, most editors and authors aren't friends. Friendly, certainly, but a relationship beyond the editorial one is rare (and trust me, for editors it's sometimes much, much harder to edit friends because often friends expect you to be even nicer and love their work even more).

But you and your editor do need a mutual respect and understanding. Sometimes editorial styles and personalities simply don't match. It happens. I'm sorry. It's hard for editors too. No one is usually at fault; you just don't mesh!

Editorial relationships don't have to last a lifetime. It's okay to outgrow an editor, to not vibe with them, to feel as if you need something or someone different in an editorial relationship.

In fact (I need all *my* authors to look away here lol), I will go so far as to suggest that it can be great if you work with different editors over your career, because you're going to learn something different from each editor. And a new editor may challenge your way of thinking about your writing in a way that hasn't been presented to you before.

(This is true, unless you're one of my authors, then you should probably stay with me forever, you'll miss me! I'll miss you!)

Joking aside, there is also something to be said for working with someone you have a history with, have established open communication with, who knows your writing quirks, understands your voice, has a knowledge of your world/stories/characters, and who you just vibe with.

Sometimes you simply don't mess with what's working and swap out just for the sake of variety.

Last, remember that not every editor who hangs out their editorial shingle is a good, qualified, or professional editor or isn't a qualified editor for *your* book. That's it, that's the comment; I don't think belaboring this point is necessary.

Do your homework, read example books, get a sample edit if they give them, and research their qualifications.

The Bottom Line

At the end of the day, the work is yours. However, keep in mind that the editor is answerable to not only you, but also to potentially their boss (the publisher) or at the very least, the reader—after all, reviews generally don't spare the editor any more than they do the author, and many readers tend to "blame" the editor when there are any problems in the work.

I can't tell you how many reviews I've seen that said "this needed better editing." Sometimes it didn't have an editor. Sometimes it didn't have a qualified editor. Sometimes the author chose not to do the edits.

Whatever the case, readers are quick to point out bad or lack of editing. But good editing? Hardly anyone ever notices, because if the editor is doing their job right, there's nothing to notice. Not many reviews say "this was so well edited", but plenty ask "where was the editor on this?"

Good editing is often invisible, and as editors, and authors doing self-edits, we need to accept, understand and embrace that as part of our role in the book.

The voice, the vision, the time investment belongs mainly to you, the author. It's okay to feel protective and territorial. Just don't let it take over and shut you off to the possibilities a good editor and a good edit can offer.

Because a good editor, with a good author, can take a book from awesome to beyond awesome (or as I like to say, thanks to Rhino from *Bolt*, take a book to be-awesome). I hope you get the opportunity to experience that.

TAKE ACTION

Make a list of what you want in an editor to give your-self not only a starting place for looking, but also an understanding of what you're looking for so you can recognize a good match for you versus a not-so-good match for you.

Ask yourself about what qualities you want in their feedback, their work structure, their work experience, their timeline and more.

Think about things like:

- What kind of editorial experience are you looking for?
- What style of feedback do you do best with?
- How open to edits are you?
- What type of personality do you need your editor to have?
- Do you need them to also be your friend, or just a business partner?

Consider checking out my resource **EditMatch: The Complete Toolkit for Choosing the Right Editor**, which includes a short workbook with a checklist to help you figure out the most important elements you would like in an editor, figure out a budget, and set yourself up for finding the best editorial match.

TIPS & TIDBITS

This comment was too interesting not to share and I couldn't figure out a way to fit it into the above text.

One of my beta readers works as a translator, and in the section on the previous page where I say *"Not many reviews say 'this was so well edited', but plenty ask 'where was the editor on this?'"*

They left this comment:

> *Yeah, same goes for translators, sadly. People only notice if we get something wrong or the translated text is a bit clunky, while the kudos go to the original author for the smoothly translated, beautifully worded text that we work hours and hours to polish.*

CHAPTER 20

HOW TO BE A GOOD CRITIQUE PARTNER, BETA READER OR EDITOR

Perhaps the most important takeaway of this chapter is that critiquing someone else's work isn't about enforcing "rules" or rewriting their voice. It's about helping make their story the best it can be for *their readers*.

TL;DR

- Your job as a critique partner is to enhance the author's voice and story, not impose your own preferences or style.
- Give balanced feedback—share what problems you're seeing but also point out what works well (and explain why for both).
- There's a difference between critique from an experienced crit partner and reviews from a reader. A good critique partner looks at how the target audience will experience the work, not just their personal reaction.

- Focus on what makes the story confusing or unclear for readers, not what you personally don't like.
- Those writing "rules" everyone loves to quote? They're suggestions, not absolutes. Use them when they help, ignore them when they don't, but don't make them the basis of your entire critique.
- Explain why something isn't working rather than just pointing out problems.
- Be diplomatic but honest—remember, there's a person behind that manuscript who's trusting you with their work. I'm all for "real" feedback but it doesn't have to be harsh!
- Check your own biases and be willing to do the work to educate yourself when needed.
- Put that ego aside as much as possible when giving (or receiving) critique. We're all here to help each other create better books.
- Set clear expectations upfront about how you'll work together—it makes everything smoother for everyone.

———

In a book about the foundations of how to self-edit, this feels like a relevant chapter to include, because understanding how to give critique to others and do it well is a skill that also translates to learning how to *accept* constructive critique and perhaps also learn how not to internalize every bit of critique or negative review.

In short, learning about giving and receiving critique in a constructive way is a kindness to yourself —and to those you're working with.

But also, this chapter is important because a good critique partner who offers thoughtful, constructive feedback is someone to treasure. I not only want you to have the tools to *be* that person for someone else, but to also be able to *find* that person and benefit from the experience.

Too many authors in the early stages of their writing journeys have come to me and said they're looking for a critique partner but have had bad experiences, or don't know how to find one but feel having a good critique partner would make a difference for them.

On the other hand, at various times, I've had a lot of authors either tell me all the things their critique partners/contest judges (and also their editors!) once told them to absolutely not do. This left them disillusioned on the experience of having or working with a critique partner (or working with an editor or entering a contest again, depending on the circumstance), and made them unsure about trying to find someone new to build a relationship with.

Hearing about these experiences always makes me feel a bit spunky on behalf of authors, and I was moved years ago to put together a list of "rules" of editing and critiquing for authors to share with their critique partners (and maybe their editors).

Of course, the word "rules" is in scare quotes because it's meant to be tongue in cheek, since we've already established my feelings about rules. But I think when you're working with critique partners especially, where there's no contract or one person in a position of "authority" so to speak, establishing expectations for behavior, critique, and how you'll work together can be helpful in avoiding misunderstandings and hurt feelings.

Too many times I've heard from people about critique partner or group experiences that are one-sided, or where someone feels they're only getting positive "this is great" comments but not helpful critique, or where one person feels they're often giving more than they're receiving.

Because of the possibility for misunderstandings, as you enter into critique relationships, communication about the process and expectations is valuable, and will lead to rewarding and long-lasting relationships.

And just as an aside: maybe this is a list that you also need to keep in mind as you edit your own work as well.

"Rules" for being an effective critique partner (or editor)

1. Just because someone has told you it's a "rule" doesn't mean it actually is (including the things in this series of books!). Writing "rules" should be considered more along the lines of well-meaning, sometimes helpful, suggestions. Please don't use writing "rules" in place of subjective feedback tailored to the person's manuscript.

2. Above all, edits and feedback should be

unique to the author and their story, not generic blanket "rules" that may not take author voice into account.

3. It's okay to use adverbs. Stop pointing out every adverb used in your crit partner's manuscript. Especially when you're probably only really pointing out the -ly words and missing all of the other adverbs. Adverbs are a necessary part of the English language, as they explain how, when, how much. Stop telling authors they can't use them.

4. Every use of "was" and "to be" is not passive. Also, passive voice isn't always bad.

5. Your job is to point out when things don't work because they're confusing, not when it's just something you don't like or isn't to your personal taste (or doesn't follow an arbitrary writing "rule").

6. If you're going to focus on a "rule" you'd better be able to explain why it's a "rule", who made it, why it has to be followed…and also make sure you actually understand the "rule".

7. Being able to explain not just that something isn't working but why it's not working is a key skill for critique partners and editors. If you can't explain why, ask yourself if what you're recommending is necessary.

8. I keep putting "rule" in quote marks because I think it's important we all understand that most "rules" are arbitrary and subjective when we're talking about non-grammar. And even the grammar stuff can be debatable as to what's exactly correct (here's where we start an argument about *'s* following *s*). We all know that the "rules" are meant to be helpful, but they're really just advice, not edicts, and like all advice, we can choose whether we want to take it or not.

9. POV changes are okay. They're even okay mid-paragraph. Don't force a break into them. Point them out when you're confused about whose head we're in, don't point them out just because they've changed. It's fine if you're a point-of-view purist in your own writing, but don't impose your preferences on someone else's book!

10. This isn't your book. Don't insert your voice into it. You have your own book for that (and if you don't, then maybe you should. But write your own, don't rewrite someone else's to your own voice.).

11. If this is your own book, you also need to respect your own voice and not edit it out of your book by following everyone else's suggestions, feedback, "rules" or criticism. Protect your voice while allowing for change and growth and improvement.

12. When we talk about voice being important, we mean that everyone has their own way of explaining, describing and writing things. People come from different backgrounds, different lived experiences, and different parts of the world. Their way is probably not your way, so don't go in and rewrite phrasing or choose new words just because that's the way *you* think they should be. That's *your* voice, not the author's.

13. Be respectful in your criticism of the author's work. We all have ego and feelings, and we should take care to not deliberately cause harm. It's okay to be critical during the critique process (it's called critique for a reason) but there's no reason to be harsh. Choose your phrasing diplomatically. Sometimes there's no way to avoid things sounding more up front; it's fine, just be aware!

14. If you're editing, be aware that it is possible for you to be wrong. Your word isn't necessarily final. And the author shouldn't always change it because you said so.

15. Be respectful in your disagreement with the author's choices. Maybe you don't like POV switches, the use of -ly adverbs, or similes. Fine, okay, but if the author chooses to use them in their work, and you've had the opportunity to point out why they may not be the strongest writing, be respectful when you disagree. If you

want to continue to explain, make sure you have reasonable explanations for your feelings. It's not a personal attack on you if they don't agree, so don't make it a personal attack on them when they don't agree with your suggestions (and please note the use of the word "suggestions").

16. Don't forget to point out what you like about their work. Tell them you love a certain line, give compliments on the emotional intensity of a moment, let them know a character is a new favorite of yours. Criticism and edits are necessary to polishing a manuscript, but so are compliments. It helps the author know they're on the right path, that they've done things well and that this book can be successful.

17. If you're editing your own work, don't forget to notice the things you love! Fall in love with your work, make a point of noticing what's great, and don't just focus on the self-criticism.

18. On the other hand, critiques that aren't critical at all and are only full of "awesome job" and "I love this book" actually aren't that helpful. You're a line of defense before the much harsher, much more critical reading world sees it. You wouldn't let your girlfriend go out into the world with her skirt tucked into her panties; don't let your author friend go out into the world with their writing oops left on the page.

19. If you expect your critique partner or author to set aside their ego while reading your comments and suggestions, shouldn't you do the same when reading their work? Ego is one of the biggest barriers to successful editing. On both sides of the equation.

20. Recognize your own bias and that your lived experiences are not the author's lived experiences. Is it possible your bias has made you ask questions or leave critique that's not necessary, that's hurtful, or that doesn't recognize cultural, ethnic, gender or other differences?

21. Before you leave a comment, make a change, or give a suggestion, ask yourself this question: is this going to make the book a better reading experience for the majority of readers, or am I just changing it to suit myself?

22. And then ask yourself this question: do I need to further educate myself before I ask this question or leave this critique?

23. Show gratitude, empathy, understanding for the person who's made themselves vulnerable and allowed you to give them feedback. Open yourself up to their questions about your critique.

24. Be as generous with your praise as you are with critique.

One rule for authors

1. Be open to the editing experience. Your writing isn't perfect right from the first draft and sometimes not even the third. Sure, you can break the rules, say you're using things because of voice, and generally leave the story exactly how you wrote it, but honestly…you're probably not that good (yeah, that was harsh, but I don't know too many authors who don't need edits/critique).

Remember what we said about ego?

Give your edits and critiques fair consideration, trying to put ego aside because ego is the thing that can be the greatest barrier in the course of edits (and learning). The harsher, much less kind reading world is up next. Let your editor and critique partners do their job and support you, make you pretty, and get you ready for the public.

Recognize that crit partners and editors are trying to be helpful, that it's okay for you to say no to suggestions, that not all edits can be phrased as nicely as we might want (sometimes being blunt is what a book needs)—and that at the end of the day, *you* have the choices!

Don't rewrite another author's work

Should you provide alternative phrasings when you're critiquing or editing?

Yes. And no. Let's start with no: don't rewrite things, because the rewrite is *your* voice, not the author's.

But yes, sometimes it's easier and more clear to offer re-phrasing or suggestions. Sometimes. Do it when it helps provide clarity for the author. Not when you just want to insert more pleasing-to-you word choices.

Say you're reading a story with repetitive sentence structures and that's getting in the way of your reading enjoyment. Instead of suggesting specific rewrites, highlight the sentences that have the repetitive structure and leave a comment that says something like, "I've highlighted these sentences to show repetitive use of this same sentence structures. Ther's a rhythm that's a bit stilted and awkward. You'll need to rewrite this section so it flows more smoothly and to avoid the repetition. If you're stuck or need suggestions for how to do this, I'm happy to offer them."

Even as a critique partner it's not your job to rewrite because your voice isn't your crit partner's voice, and your voice isn't better than their voice just because you recognized the problem—it only means you have the distance to see what's going on.

You should point out the trouble areas, not rewrite them to suit yourself.

Having someone rewrite things can be a big issue for authors who don't have a strong sense of their own voice and then work with crit partners who rewrite instead of suggest. The experience of being rewritten like this can result in what we call "voice killing" and end up causing writing paralysis, writer's block, and a general insecurity over their own voice and writing abilities.

On the other hand, if your critique partner asks for help, suggestions, or you can provide one example in an area that says "here's what I mean", that's not rewriting, that's showing and that is different. Do that. Not for the whole book, though.

They're just not my reader

Sometimes I see authors tell other authors that if someone (a critique partner, beta reader, editor or reader) didn't like their book it means "they're just not your reader".

Sure, that can be true but it's a whole lot more nuanced than that.

It's a handy excuse to pull out, it can be something easy to say to dismiss critique, and it can also fall under the category of toxic positivity, but it's not necessarily true that someone "isn't your reader" if they don't like your book.

First, I want to take this moment to clarify critique versus review.

In short, a good critique partner (or editor) who offers feedback isn't the same as a reader leaving a review. Sometimes the readers who leave reviews genuinely *aren't* your reader. And sometimes the reviews a reader leaves can offer helpful feedback even though reviews are for readers, not authors.

What you want to be cautious of is lumping a qualified critique partner (or editor) in with someone who's a reader.

Why?

Okay, first, let me call back to Chapter 9, where I talk about the difference between beta readers and professional editors. That information pertains here as well.

Like a professional editor, presumably your critique partner has (or should have) some greater level of authority in their feedback than the general reading public because you've chosen the crit partner based on their qualifications. You're going to assume they know more about the craft of writing, and general publishing, than a reader.

That said, the *key difference* is that like your editor, you want your critique partner to give feedback based not just on how they're experiencing your work but also based on how they believe your market—your target readership—will experience your work.

Your CP's goal should be to aid you in creating the best reading experience possible for your market and your target reader.

A reader leaving a review is nine times out of ten going to only offer feedback based on their own *individual experience* with your work. Their goal with their review is to share, with other readers, how they experienced the book with other readers. Do they hope the author reads it? I don't know, maybe some do. But crowdsourcing edits on your work via reviews is a whole other topic!

So calling back to "not my reader", I want to emphasize that it's good to remember that of course you can't take every critique (or review) to heart, or think that you need to take action on every single piece of feedback you get, because that would/can be so damaging:

I know authors who've paralyzed their writing skills because they've read and listened to every critique.

But I don't want you to use "not my reader" to always sweep aside critique, especially if it's a thoughtful critique from someone you've chosen to work with, if it's being said more than once by different people, or if it's someone whose opinion you trust or who you know has experience giving critique or gauging the reader experience/publishing market.

If you keep saying "not my reader" when you get critique, you may be losing an opportunity for writing growth.

And there are *always* opportunities for writing growth.

TAKE ACTION

Creating a system for good communication and clear expectations is going to be vital for developing a healthy, useful, and transformative critique partner relationship.

So many authors think having a critique relationship means you simply send the person your work and ask for feedback. But that approach, without expectations or specific requests, is just as likely to end in disappointment or an experience that doesn't give you helpful feedback.

Instead, when you start working with someone new, establish some good boundaries and expectations. Set up your communication so you each know what the other needs, what you expect, and what will make this work the best for you.

Put together a document with a few guidelines for your critique partners or have a conversation with them to set some up, so you know you're all on the same page.

It's never too late! You also have my permission to share the "Rules" for Being an Effective Critique Partner (or Editor) above with a small group of your crit partners, if that makes it easier! (Just don't post them to large groups or on the Internet or pass them around, please!)

TIPS & TIDBITS

When I talk about not crowdsourcing your edits, this can refer to a few things—how many beta readers you use, how much confidence you have in making decisions about your story, asking your writing group to weigh in on your editor's every suggestion…those are all types of crowdsourcing edits. At some point, you need to gain the confidence to write and edit with a small, core team whose input you trust.

However, the other thing I mean when I talk about crowdsourcing edits is using reviews, whether pre- or post-publication, to edit your book or impact future books.

I'm not suggesting that you not read reviews, as I think the decision to read or not read reviews is individual to each other.

What I do want, is to suggest caution when reading reviews and then immediately thinking "Oh no, this thing that this one reviewer (or ARC reviewer) pointed out is something I need to change immediately."

Recently, I had an author who had a book that was in the ARC (Advanced Reader Copy) stage and two reviews mentioned something they had misunderstood/misread/missed. The author had a bit of a panic attack and wondered if she needed to do another editing pass, but we both went and looked and...the issue was simply not there. This was a case where it proved it's just not possible to write for every reader, and to control how every reader interprets your story.

When you start crowdsourcing your edits via reviews, you're allowing hundreds and sometimes thousands of voices and visions for the story into the editing process, and that's going to make it difficult, if not impossible, to preserve *your voice* and *your vision* because everyone is going to review based on what they like best and what they want in a story.

The moral of this tidbit is that you need to have confidence in yourself as an author, along with the team you're working with, and remember that you and your editor are editing for more than one person.

Or, as I saw one author put it, paraphrased, "Thanks for tagging me in your review telling me all the ways I need to write different and change my story, but I have an editor I trust and pay to do that."

SECTION FIVE
YOUR NEXT STEPS (AKA THE END OF THIS BOOK BUT THE BEGINNING OF YOUR EDITS)

CHAPTER 21
WRITING AND EDITING A BOOK ON WRITING AND EDITING IS META

TL;DR

- Some things are evergreen and that includes most of the advice I've put together over the years on how to edit a book. The other thing that's evergreen? Embracing the realization that "perfect" is a myth.

———

The process of editing this book became one that felt extremely meta at times. You may notice that I include mentions of my own beta readers, that I mention and address comments they left, and that some of the Tips & Tidbits questions and comments came from those same beta readers.

Usually, you don't break the fourth wall, so to speak, quite like this in a book. Edits and comments are meant to be invisible to the reader, right?

But I found that I didn't want a book about editing to not actually address my own process of going through edits and beta reading.

It felt...right, to include mentions of my own editing process throughout a book about editing and acknowledge that the process I'm encouraging you to use is the same process I used—even if you may be editing fiction and I'm editing non-fiction.

While editing fiction and non-fiction have some noticeable differences, there's also a lot of overlap, especially in the mindset around how you approach and interact with edits and the people offering you feedback.

So I'm going to share some of what I went through while writing and editing this book in hopes that it will help you see that you're not alone in your thoughts, feelings, frustrations and roadblocks!

In fact, I experienced many of the same emotions and mental blocks and struggles that you have probably experienced during your own publishing journey.

Maybe it would make you feel better to know that I struggled many, many times while writing and editing this book. Some of it flowed so easily and some of it I labored over. I had periods of extreme anxiety about whether I was doing justice to a topic, being clear enough, giving enough actionable takeaways.

And I spent actual years (no, that is not an exaggeration) thinking about how I was representing inclusivity in writing and editing. Did I include enough information to get authors started? Did I get anything wrong, use poor phrasing? Was I going to get negative reviews and comments about those portions of the book?

I also spent months avoiding edits and rewrites on this book, missing my own self-imposed deadlines, because for a period of time I was *over* it. I mean, in theory this book had been in the making for about sixteen years, so perhaps I had good reason to be a bit burnt out on it, but also…it's just something that happens sometimes during the creation journey.

But taking my own advice on getting distance and setting it aside worked to help renew my creative energies and give me new insight into the sections I was struggling with and needed a little more oomph behind.

I also found myself trying to avoid using my own recommended framework, and trying to do proofreading before I did beta reads and line edits (honestly, I'm still not sure what I was thinking). I may have also a time or two thought about just skipping steps or telling myself "I can do that later".

I managed to rein myself back in, because I know, *I know,* that each step is important, and doing them in order is also important, and I'm glad I eventually listened to myself.

I also absolutely, for sure read this book with a critical eye as I prepared it for its final proofreading, half convinced I was going to just scrap the whole thing.

Yet, while there were a few thoughts I had about the book during edits, none of them were "this advice is terrible and I don't know what I'm talking about."

In fact, during the course of the *at least* half dozen times I read this book and the hundreds of hours spent on edits, I was reminded repeatedly of how much sheer practical, good advice I'd put together over the years.

And I was proud of myself.

That's the experience I want you to have with your writing and editing journey as well.

I want you to be proud of your journey, proud of your book, and proud of yourself. And one way to get there is to remember that no matter where you're at in your writing and editing journey, whether you're just beginning or you're twenty years in, having a process, a place to start and a place to end is always going to make completing a book easier.

And slightly less likely to want to set it all on fire by the end, lol!

I also realized, while editing this book, that a lot of this advice is evergreen. *Before You Hit Send*®, the course, started in 2010 and nearly all of the basic information and lessons from that course still exist. Some of them are in this book, some will appear in later books.

Of course I've mentioned that I had to update over the years, and there have been revisions, a few things I've walked back or changed my mind about, a significant amount of careful attention to microaggressions, and so many things I've learned and added.

But the foundational information has remained consistent and evergreen.

It reminded me that though publishing is moving and changing faster than ever, and it feels like there's never enough time to keep up with marketing, social media, advertising, promotions...one thing always stays the same: writing and editing the book are still the most important activities you can do in your publishing career.

Without a good book, without a good story that delivers a memorable reading experience, the rest is going to be meaningless. When all else fails, come back to your writing and editing foundations.

The other thing that I experienced as I was editing this book was a reminder of how often authors enter edits with the idea of "perfect" in mind.

As I said earlier in this chapter, I absolutely encountered moments of doubt while editing and periods of "ugh, I hate this". (Even being an editor, I have moments of hating edits, it's pretty standard!) There were times when I struggled to find the words or phrasing or articulate what I wanted to say in a way that felt as if it would be helpful—because above all I want this book to be helpful.

But the one thing I never thought as I edited this book was *it has to be perfect*.

You would think, as an editor, "perfect" would be my goal. Instead, one of the things I embrace and encourage my authors to embrace is the idea that there is no perfect. It doesn't exist and chasing it can create some of the worst anxiety and inability to let go of a project.

I was chuckling to myself at one point, after having the book proofread several times, because I knew, despite that, there would still be plenty of errors and typos for people to point out. And I was chuckling because, in my experience as an editor and long-time content creator, people do seem to take a special joy in feeling a "gotcha" moment in letting an editor know they spotted a mistake in something the editor has created.

Then I realized that some of that comes because authors have been told to strive for a mythical "perfect" rather than striving for the best possible reading experience in terms of content, not commas.

I've said it before but as we wrap up this particular book, I'll say it again: commas can be important, but one thing authors and editors often lose sight of is that it's not the comma that's going to create a compulsively readable, unputdownable, fall-in-love-and-recommend-to-everyone book.

It's the story, the characters, the journey that your readers are going to love and remember.

Or in the case of non-fiction, like this book, the content, the takeaways, the ability to implement and put it to use.

I don't believe in perfection, I don't expect perfection, and I hope you can lean into that too!

There is no "perfect" in publishing and if you can let go of that standard, you'll free yourself from the anxiety of achieving the impossible to instead focus more on the joy of creation and the reader's experience with the story and the characters.

CHAPTER 22
NOW WHAT?

Easy, now you edit!

Kidding! I know that diving into editing isn't that easy, and things can still seem overwhelming and confusing.

Plus, you might still be wondering how to edit and what to edit.

While this book was meant to lay the foundation of editing for you, later books in this series will go into detail about the specifics of editing your book, from developmental edits to proofreading.

In the meantime, here are a few suggested ways to get started:

1. Use the Editing Checklist and Style Guide template that I've included in Appendices C and D, or download them from my website.

2. Open them / put them into a document (yes, that's a step).

3. Familiarize yourself with the content of the editing checklist and think about what writing or story issues seem to pop up the most for you (what comments your critique partners make, your editor, or things you've already noticed in your own writing).

4. Add those items to your checklist to start with first!

5. Set clear, manageable and practical goals for editing. Don't set goals based on what you think you should accomplish; set goals based on what's practical for you to accomplish.

6. Find an editing support system. This might look like a writing group, critique partners, beta readers, or editors. Working with others gives you greater insight into your own writing, as well as your editing needs.

7. If it all feels overwhelming, start with one thing. Not the commas (sorry), but focus on just one aspect of the story. The first page, the first scene, the last chapter, the meet cute, the moment the mystery comes to light...it can be anything, but just focus on that part of the book.

8. Now make a list of parts to focus on, breaking the editing down into one manageable piece at a time. There's no reason to think of it as a whole if it feels like too much.

9. Listen. Go back to Chapter 4 on listening and use that lesson to start the editing process.

10. Do it the way that works for you. As I was writing this chapter and had quite literally *just* written point #9, one of my clients messaged me and wondered if they were letting their readers down by not following a particular recommendation in the editing process.

And my response to them feels like the perfect way to end this chapter and this book because I think it's something every author needs to hear:

"Not at all. Not every tip is going to work for every writer. You do it in the way that works for you to get it done in the way that's not just best for the book, but best for you."

———

Coming Next in *The Edit Your Way* Series

Edit Your Way: Fix the Story

Pre-order now and take control of your story-level edits.

Find the link on the *Edit Your Way Resources* page at angelajames.co/resources.

NOTE ON LINKS

In this book, I reference different resources. Because of the difficulty of linking to resources in a book, I've provided a resource page on my website. If you want to interact with any of the additional resources or sources I provide, please visit my website and head to the *Edit Your Way Resources* page at angelajames.co/resources.

ACKNOWLEDGMENTS

These aren't written yet.

See that line? That line indicated the last blank space in this manuscript. The last thing I had to fill in and I was avoiding it.

I don't know about you, but I love to read the acknowledgments and see who helped along the way and what the author has to say about it.

Because I'm continuing on in the vein of a book about editing being meta, I'll just share that I absolutely dreaded writing these. Not because I don't feel immensely grateful but because I love acknowledgments and I wanted them to be special and perfect.

But as we learned through this book, nothing is ever perfect, so I'll just settle for them being special.

The number of people who've given me support on this project—both on the book in particular but also for *Before You Hit Send*® and my entire career in general as well, which has made this book possible—is absolutely as long as my arm. So I'm going to end up leaving someone out and I'm sorry for it.

And yet, these acknowledgments are going to be long because there's a lot of people to name!

I'm going to start by thanking my mom, Mary Jean Roehrich Maixner, who passed away when I was 17 but who, in the time I had her with me, instilled in me a towering love of books and reading that has shaped my life.

While I first fell in love with reading Nancy Drew and Trixie Belden, I truly fell in love with the romance genre when I started "borrowing" the Harlequin category romances that she kept in a brown grocery bag next to her recliner when I was in fourth grade and reading them under the covers by flashlight at night. Of course Mom knew, but she never once tried to moderate or limit my reading, including when I moved on to Sidney Sheldon and Stephen King in 6th grade.

Everything I've done in my career exists because she loved me that much.

This book was dedicated to my husband but I also need to acknowledge that he didn't know I was writing a book until I announced it publicly. I guess I didn't tell him I was writing a book? Oops! This is probably worse than Taylor Swift forgetting to tell Ed Sheeran she was engaged before announcing it publicly, right? But once he found out (my husband, not Ed), he was so excited to share about it.

And one day, a few weeks after he found out about the book, we were sitting at a bar talking to a complete stranger about publishing and I wish I could have recorded my husband talking about my editing philosophies and the book I was writing. It was…everything. My wish for you all is to have one person in your life who cheerleads you that way, with wholehearted enthusiasm, love and complete and utter belief in your awesomeness. Thanks, babe.

As it happens, I'm very fortunate to have another

guy in my life who's just about as equally as enthusiastic about my business and what we do. In fact, my assistant, Dan, described himself to my ARC team as "the second biggest *Edit Your Way* fan after AJ's husband" and he's not wrong. Dan is such a huge, integral part of my business, and I'm super grateful to him every single day, for all he does for me and for our clients. Dan also helped with many different parts of this book process, from formatting to the resource page to getting it up for sale on my website, to helping me make some decisions when I had decision fatigue, plus helping me with a whole lot of other moving parts. So when I say the book wouldn't exist without him, that's a real, factual statement. You're the best, Dan!

Of course, I have to say thank you to my other family who lives with me, my daughter, Bri, and my brother, Adam, for always being proud of me. Love you, both!

Thanks to two people who worked on early versions of *Before You Hit Send*®, my friend of 20 years, Patricia Brittingham, who worked as my early assistant on the course and who, when I announced the book said, "This is amazing news! I remember the workshop, *Before You Hit Send*®. I was in awe and proud of you then and I knew back then at some point you would write a book," and my former assistant at Samhain Publishing, Imogen Howson, who years after we worked together there, helped me proofread all of the BYHS lessons (several times). As you can tell, I've really lucked out in the assistant department over the years, and like with many others I'm thanking, this book could not have become a book without their help.

Much thanks to the cheer, patience and tenacity of my final proofreader, Sharon Muha, who went over the book for me several times and also kept on me, "When are you going to finish the book and send it to me?" in a very encouraging way because she knew I was procrastinating. For months. You're the best, Sharon! (Not for nothing, Sharon is a proofreader for hire if you're looking for someone...) Any errors I missed are not because Sharon didn't do her job, but because I didn't do mine!

I owe so much gratitude that it makes me want to cry for how much I lucked out working with Kharma Kelley who I hired to read parts of this book for comments on writing and editing for inclusivity. I've said it before, but this was the hardest part of this book to write and I was never going to publish it without getting some expert advice. Words probably will *never* express how grateful I am to Kharma for her input. I learned so much from her in the process. She provided me feedback in very clear, thorough ways, gave me areas of praise that I desperately needed to hear at that stage of revising those pages, and then she generously offered me the opportunity to give you her Inclusive Heart Test as an appendix in this book. Working with her was one of the best decisions I've ever made. Thank you, thank you, Kharma! Please do consider using Kharma if you're looking for a sensitivity reader. And as with all parts of this book, if there's anything I got wrong, missed or left out, it's completely my responsibility.

Alongside Kharma, I would be super remiss if I didn't thank a specific group of people I worked with once upon a time. We were tasked with creating a guide to editing for diversity (that was the literal name of the task we were given, just to be clear) and we worked together for almost 2 years on a project that, while it was never seen by the audience it was intended for, changed me profoundly because of the people who I worked on it with. These co-workers of mine gave so selflessly of their time, their knowledge, their emotional energy and their sheer care. They will never be properly appreciated for all of that, but I'll always remember.

Many, many thanks to my beta readers, who read an earlier version of this book what ended up being 18 months before I actually published the dang thing. Their feedback helped shape the version you see now, and it's some of their comments that allowed me to make this a bit more of a meta experience, giving you a peek behind the curtains of editing a book and working with beta readers. Thanks goes to all of these people for their time and effort in reading through the book and leaving such amazing feedback: Deana Kussman, Kim Findlay, Landra Graf, Laura J, Stephanie Cranford, Barbara Lucas, Edith Lalonde, Christi Snow, Helen J. Conway, Meg Napier, Amber Sumner, Cara Dion, Anna Richland.

Thank you to the authors who trusted me enough to reach out and offer snippets of their work for the chapter on voice, even though all they had to go on was the prompt and my assurance that I wasn't using their work for evil. That took a lot of trust, and I appreciate them helping me help you. Thank you, Caty Rogan, Thien-Kim Lam, Rafe Jadison, Blaine D. Arden, B.

Benford, Helen J. Conway, Liv Macy, Marie Tuhart, and Piper J. Drake.

Oh my gosh, there were so many people who volunteered to be on my ARC team and spent a few months watching in real time as I detailed the final processes of editing and publishing a book, that I can't name them all right here, but as those of you who are authors know, ARC readers are integral to the publishing process and I'm so happy to have people who were interested enough in this book to volunteer. Thank you!!!!

There are two people who I should thank, but their names have been lost in my memory. Thank you to the person who first asked me if I'd do a workshop for their RWA chapter on editing. I ended up creating and teaching that first version of what would become *Before You Hit Send®* on a Yahoo group, thanks to you, and your request changed the trajectory of my career for the better! And thank you to the person who once upon a time suggested the name "Before You Hit Send". Though I chose to go a different route with this book's title, that name lives on and is still one of my favorite things.

Thanks to the members of my Success Alliance community (now called The Acknowledgements for just this reason), most of whom have been with me for the past 3 years as I worked on finally producing this book, and commiserated with me as I went through the process of writing and editing—and trying to find a second professional proofreader who wouldn't ghost me, who had a website that wasn't full of typos, or who didn't suddenly change their prices mid-quote and require me to use ChatGPT to work out exactly what the fee was (for real). They all valiantly didn't laugh at me experiencing what so many authors experience, they were all as enthusiastic for me publishing a book as they've been for each other, and they have made Discord my favorite place to be and chatting. Thanks to each and every one of you for making my business strong and for sticking with me.

I also have a group of friends that I made in publishing, we've been friends for 20 years, we chat every day, sometimes we vacation together, we know each other's partners, family and children, and we've literally built careers in publishing together. They're the ones who held me together over multiple job changes and roller-coasters over the years, and who've answered my questions, supported me and been my constants. Thanks will never be enough for Shannon Stacey, Jaci Burton, Sarah Wendell, HelenKay Dimon, Vivian Arend and Laura Bradford. I hope they know they're stuck with me for life.

And these acknowledgments wouldn't be complete without thanking every author I've worked with over the years. There are quite literally thousands of you, but I learned something from each one of you, so you're all in this book, in one way or another, because it's thanks to my work with you that I know all of the things I'm passing on here, and that I share in other areas of my business. Every word of this book is thanks to you.

Last, thanks to you, the author reading this book, and to every author who's ever written and published a story. Your stories have carried me through 5 decades of life, and it's because of your books that I've been able to survive some of the hardest moments.

Your stories are a steady light in the darkest times.

Publishing a book is an act of bravery, and I appreciate every single one of you who've taken that leap of courage in order to share your stories with the world. Thank you.

SECTION SIX
APPENDICES

APPENDIX A:
ALTERNATE PATHS
THROUGH THIS BOOK

If you aren't a linear reader but more of a "find a different path" type, then here are a few alternate ways of reading this book.

While reading this book from front to back is the most comprehensive learning experience, obviously, I know sometimes it's easier to jump around in a book like this!

To help you do that, these roadmaps offer alternative paths that I've curated with specific goals and experience levels in mind.

Each roadmap guides you through the chapters most relevant to the immediate needs of the specific stated goal.

Here are the 8 roadmaps I've compiled to help you dive in:

Roadmap 1: The Quick-Start Editing Checklist Builder
Roadmap 2: Editing with Inclusivity in Mind

———

ROADMAP 1: THE QUICK-START EDITING CHECKLIST BUILDER

Goal:

Authors who want to jump straight into creating their personalized editing checklist and start editing immediately.

Path:

1. **Chapter 2: Creating Expectations**
Understand what this book offers and set your mindset.

2. **Chapter 10: Your Editing Checklist—The Most Important Part of Your Process**
The core chapter for building your checklist.

3. **Chapter 9: Edit Stages Defined**
Learn the different editing stages to organize your checklist.

4. Chapter 11: Where to Start Edits
Know where to begin applying your checklist.

5. Chapter 12: How Long Should Edits Take?
AKA How Do I Know When I'm Done Editing?
Understand when to stop.

6. Chapter 4: Quick Win—Listen or Read Aloud
Implement an immediate, powerful editing technique.

7. Chapter 22: Now What?
Plan your next steps.

Quick explanation:

This roadmap focuses on the practical mechanics of creating an editing process. It will help you build your checklist quickly and understand how to use it effectively. Once you've completed your first round of edits using this approach, I highly recommend you return to also read about voice, inclusivity, and emotional resilience.

ROADMAP 2: EDITING WITH INCLUSIVITY IN MIND

Goal:

Authors and editors committed to creating inclusive content and understanding how to edit with sensitivity and awareness.

Path:

1. **Chapter 1: Why Editing Sucks But is Important**
Ground yourself in the purpose of editing.

2. **Chapter 2: Creating Expectations**
Set the framework for learning.

3. **Chapter 8: Editing for Inclusivity**
The central chapter for this focus.

4. **Chapter 6: Author Voice**
Understand how voice intersects with inclusive language.

5. **Chapter 7: Eff the Writing "Rules"**
Learn when to break rules for authentic, inclusive storytelling.

6. **Chapter 10: Your Editing Checklist—The Most Important Part of Your Process**
Add inclusivity checks to your process.

7. **Chapter 20: How to Be a Good Critique Partner, Beta Reader or Editor**
Apply inclusive practices in collaborative relationships.

8. **Chapter 13: Using an Author Style Guide and Story Bible**
Document your inclusivity decisions.

9. **Chapter 22: Now What?**
Continue your inclusivity journey.

Quick Explanation:

This roadmap centers on the principles and practices of inclusive editing. By understanding voice, questioning traditional rules, and building inclusivity into your checklist and style guide, you create a sustainable practice that honors diverse perspectives and experiences.

ROADMAP 3: FOR EXPERIENCED AUTHORS

Goal:

Authors who have edited multiple books but want to refine their process, overcome sticking points, or level up their craft.

Path:

1. **Chapter 3: Angela's Key Principles of Editing and Other Important Thoughts**
Align with core editing philosophy.

2. **Chapter 5: The Emotional Journey of Editing**
Address the psychological challenges you may be facing.

3. **Chapter 6: Author Voice**
Deepen your understanding of your unique voice.

4. **Chapter 7: Eff the Writing "Rules"**
Gain confidence in breaking rules intentionally.

5. **Chapter 12: How Long Should Edits Take? AKA How Do I Know When I'm Done Editing?**
Solve the "when am I done?" problem.

6. **Chapter 10: Your Editing Checklist—The Most Important Part of Your Process**
Refine or rebuild your checklist.

7. **Chapter 13: Using an Author Style Guide and Story Bible**
Establish consistency across your body of work.

8. **Chapter 19: Editor-Author (and Other Team Members) Relationship(s)**
Improve collaboration with your editing team.

9. **Chapter 21: Writing and Editing a Book on Writing and Editing is Meta**
Reflect on the meta-aspects of the craft.

Quick Explanation:

This roadmap acknowledges your experience and focuses on refinement rather than basics. It addresses the emotional and philosophical aspects of editing that become more important as you mature in your craft, while providing tools to optimize your existing process.

ROADMAP 4: FOR BEGINNING AUTHORS

Goal:

New authors or those editing their first book who need a complete understanding of the editing process from the ground up.

Path:

1. **Chapter 1: Why Editing Sucks But is Important**
Understand the value of editing.

2. **Chapter 2: Creating Expectations**
Know what to expect from this book.

3. **Chapter 3: Angela's Key Principles of Editing and Other Important Thoughts**
Build your editing philosophy.

Quick Explanation:

This roadmap provides a tiered learning experience that builds knowledge progressively. It balances editing concepts with practical skills, ensuring you have both the mindset and the tools to edit effectively. The technical chapters are included early to prevent common beginner mistakes.

ROADMAP 5: DEVELOPING VOICE AND STYLE

Goal:

Authors who want to strengthen their author voice, develop consistent character voices, and make intentional stylistic choices.

Path:

1. **Chapter 2: Creating Expectations**
Set your learning framework.

2. **Chapter 6: Author Voice**
The cornerstone chapter for this focus.

3. **Chapter 7: Eff the Writing "Rules"**
Learn when to break rules to serve your voice.

Why this path works:

This roadmap prioritizes the development and preservation of your unique voice throughout the editing process. By understanding voice first, then learning how to document and protect it through style guides and checklists, you ensure that editing enhances rather than diminishes your distinctive authorial presence.

ROADMAP 6: LEARNING THE TECH TOOLS OF EDITING

Goal:

Authors who are comfortable with editing concepts but need to master the technical tools and workflows to edit more efficiently.

Path:

1. **Chapter 14: Which Word Processing Program to Use in Edits**
Choose the right tool.

2. **Chapter 15: Editing with Microsoft Word—Track Changes**
Master revision tracking.

3. **Chapter 16: Editing with Microsoft Word—Find and Replace**
Learn powerful search techniques.

4. **Chapter 17: Editing with Microsoft Word—Customizing the Quick Access Toolbar**
Optimize your workspace.

5. **Chapter 18: Backing Up Your Work**
Implement safety protocols.

6. **Chapter 10: Your Editing Checklist—The Most Important Part of Your Process**
Integrate tools into your process.

7. **Chapter 11: Where to Start Edits**
Apply tools strategically.

8. **Chapter 13: Using an Author Style Guide and Story Bible**
Use tools to maintain consistency.

9. **Chapter 22: Now What?**
Continue optimizing your workflow.

Quick Explanation:

This roadmap is practical and tool-focused. It assumes you understand why editing matters and focuses on making you proficient with the software and systems that will make your editing faster and more effective. The later chapters connect these tools to your broader editing process.

ROADMAP 7: COLLABORATING WITH A TEAM

Goal:

Authors who work with editors, critique partners, or beta readers and want to improve those relationships and get better feedback.

Path:

1. **Chapter 2: Creating Expectations**
Understand the editing framework.

2. **Chapter 9: Edit Stages Defined**
Know what type of feedback to request at each stage.

3. **Chapter 19: Editor-Author (and Other Team Members) Relationship(s)**
Build strong collaborative relationships.

4. **Chapter 20: How to Be a Good Critique Partner, Beta Reader or Editor**
Understand both sides of the relationship.

5. **Chapter 15: Editing with Word—Track Changes**
Communicate effectively through tracked changes.

6. **Chapter 13: Using an Author Style Guide and Story Bible**
Share your style decisions with collaborators.

7. **Chapter 5: The Emotional Journey of Editing**
Manage feedback emotionally.

8. **Chapter 10: Your Editing Checklist—The Most Important Part of Your Process**
Share your process with your team.

9. **Chapter 22: Now What?**
Build your editing team.

Quick Explanation:

This roadmap emphasizes the idea that editing is often a collaborative process. By understanding the different editing stages, building strong relationships, and communicating effectively through tools and documentation, you create a productive editing process that elevates your work through multiple perspectives.

ROADMAP 8: EDITING MINDSET

Goal:

Authors who struggle with the emotional challenges of editing, including perfectionism, imposter syndrome, or difficulty letting go.

Path:

1. **Chapter 1: Why Editing Sucks But is Important**
Validate your feelings about editing.

2. **Chapter 5: The Emotional Journey of Editing**
The central chapter for this focus.

3. **Chapter 3: Angela's Key Principles of Editing and Other Important Thoughts**
Build a healthy editing philosophy.

4. **Chapter 12: How Long Should Edits Take? AKA How Do I Know When I'm Done Editing?**
Learn to recognize completion.

5. **Chapter 7: Eff the Writing "Rules"**
Release perfectionism around arbitrary rules.

6. **Chapter 6: Author Voice**
Trust your unique voice.

7. **Chapter 10: Your Editing Checklist—The Most Important Part of Your Process**
Create structure to reduce anxiety.

8. **Chapter 19: Editor-Author (and Other Team Members) Relationship(s)**
Build supportive relationships.

9. **Chapter 21: Writing and Editing a Book on Writing and Editing is Meta**
Gain perspective on the process.

10. **Chapter 22: Now What?**
Move forward with confidence.

Quick Explanation:

This roadmap addresses the psychological and emotional barriers that often prevent authors from editing (and writing) effectively or completing their edits. By building emotional resilience, establishing clear boundaries, and creating supportive structures, you can edit with greater confidence and less anxiety.

A FINAL NOTE ABOUT THESE ROADMAPS

You may find that you resonate with multiple roadmaps. In that case, consider combining elements from different paths or completing one roadmap before moving to another.

Remember that these roadmaps are suggestions, not rigid requirements. Your unique needs and learning style should guide your journey through this book.

The goal of this book, and the roadmaps, is to make the content accessible and actionable for you, wherever you are in your editing journey.

APPENDIX B: 5-PASS EDITING METHOD

As mentioned in Chapter 11, this can be found as a full free download on my website, but here's an overview of the key parts of this editing method.

THE 5 PASSES AT A GLANCE

1. **Big Picture** → Story structure, character arcs, plot.
2. **Scene-Level** → Individual scene function and flow.
3. **Line Editing** → Sentence clarity, rhythm, voice.
4. **Copy Editing** → Consistency, grammar, details.
5. **Final Polish** → Formatting, typos, final cleanup.

You don't have to do all five passes. Choose what your manuscript needs right now.

YOUR APPROACH TO SELF-EDITS *MIGHT* LOOK LIKE THIS

Editing your book doesn't have to feel like spaghetti-flinging chaos. You're allowed to make a plan. In fact, it helps if you have a plan.

This is a flexible, five-layered editing approach that builds momentum without requiring you to fix every-thing all at once. You don't need to follow this in strict order—but it gives you a roadmap so you always know what's next.

Important Notes:

- This is broken down into five passes for structure, but you may need more than five passes.
- You may find that you turn some of these passes over to an editor who combines them.
- Most authors make multiple passes—that's how editing works.
- Focus is how you're going to achieve your editing results.

1. First Pass: Big Picture

This is the "zoomed out" structural story pass.

This ensures you have a cohesive story as a whole that's delivering the story you want to tell. Here you're going to be looking at those big-picture elements that ensure a magical reading experience for your reader, nailing story arc, world-building, characterization, relationship development, plot and more.

Focus:

You're looking at the important story elements here. Think overall story:

- Relationship development
- Characterization
- World-building
- Plot
- The beginning
- The end
- Character arcs
- Overall story goals

Look for gaps in motivation or emotion, underdeveloped character arcs, or unresolved subplots.

Ask:

- Is the story I meant to tell showing up on page?
- Do my characters have clear motivation, clear growth, clear conflict?
- Is the relationship progression clear on page?
- Are there story threads that get lost or does the timeline get muddy?
- Do I have a satisfying ending?

Tip:

Don't stop to fix sentences here. Resist the urge to move into the tiny tweaks stage. Make notes instead. Stay zoomed out. Fixing the sentences is the easy part and your brain will try to trick you and default to that, telling you that you're making significant editing inroads because you're fixing typos and rewriting sentences.

2. Second Pass: Scene-Level Work

Zoom in on individual scene function and flow

Once your story foundation is solid, you want to zoom in on the next layer, looking more closely at a scene by scene level. Identifying how each scene's function and flow are working, how each is pulling its weight in the story. What is each scene doing (or not doing) in the story?

You want your scenes to do things like move the story forward (every scene does NOT have to move the story arc forward, that's just one purpose), build the relationship, enhance characterization, add to the world-building, deepen the story emotion or enhance reader enjoyment.

Focus:

- Deep point of view
- Pacing
- Timeline
- Arcs (story, relationship, pacing)
- Emotional connection
- Emotional payoff
- Hooks

Check for info-dumps, saggy sections, or disjointed flow.

Look for repetition, inconsistent tone, or pacing issues between scenes. You might end up cutting, combining, or reordering scenes here.

Ask:

- What is this scene doing in the story and is it in the right place (and the right POV)?
- Does it move the plot, relationship, characterization forward?
- Does it reveal something important to the reader about the character, story, mystery, world-building, relationship?
- Is there internal or external conflict present (does there need to be?)
- Does the pacing feel tight—as in, meaningful things are happening on page—or does it drag?

Tip:

Read your manuscript scene by scene—not just chapter by chapter. Jot down the purpose of each scene in the margin or a tracker. This helps you spot flat scenes that exist just to "get to the next thing," and makes it easier to combine or cut without losing emotional impact.

3. Third Pass: Line Editing

Zoom in to sentence-level clarity, rhythm, and voice.

This is the part where your writing starts to *sound* like you—and where your characters start to sound like *themselves*. You're shaping the flow of each line, tightening repetition, and making your sentences make sense in the book, cutting those that don't belong, and expanding those that need more texture.

Focus:

This is worth repeating: clarity, rhythm, and voice.

- Trim repetition.
- Strengthen weak sentence structure or repetitive sentence structure.
- Deepen POV.
- Add blocking.
- Tweak dialogue.
- Fix overwriting.

- Look for where you can combine sentences or fix sentence fragments.
- Or maybe you're going to separate sentences and add sentence fragments.

This is about leaning into both your author voice and your characters' voices, and you're massaging the actual writing instead of the story elements.

Ask:

- Does each sentence sound like it belongs to this character or narrator?
- Am I repeating myself—or writing around what I mean?
- Have I defaulted to vague phrasing or passivity?
- Do my transitions and beats feel natural?
- Is there energy and variation in how the prose moves?
- Am I varying my sentence structure?

Tip:

Use a read-aloud tool (or your own voice!) for this pass. Your ear will catch what your eyes miss. And try searching your manuscript for common crutch words or filter phrases ("I feel," "he saw," "just," "that")—this can help you focus your edits and stay efficient. Save a "line edit" word list of your most common issues and do a search/replace pass.

4. Fourth Pass: The Details

Zooooming in on technical clarity and internal consistency.

The devil is in the details (that's a cliche saying, in case you're looking for some figurative language) but the copy editing stage is where some of the most obvious errors are caught.

This fourth pass is about the details. Making sure you're following your own style guide. The characters' eyes don't change color. The timeline is as perfect as you can get it. Names don't change.

Think of this as now moving into cleanup mode. This pass is about technical clarity and internal consistency—not just grammar, but continuity, naming, formatting, and anything that could trip up a reader's immersion. You're not rewriting here—you're verifying. Think of this as the detail pass that strengthens the polish. This stage is where having a style guide for yourself as an author, or having a series style guide, can really come in handy!

Focus:

Accuracy, consistency, and clarity.

- You're double-checking names, dates, ages, timelines, and style choices.
- This is where you fix dangling modifiers, if you missed them in the line edit stage.
- Sort out punctuation.

- Clean up overused tags or formatting quirks.

It's also where you decide:

- Am I consistently using em dashes?
- Is internal thought formatted the same way throughout? (Remember, internal dialogue is first person, present tense, italics.)

Ask:

- Is character info consistent (age, description, backstory)?
- Are timelines or events in the right sequence?
- Am I consistent in how I use punctuation, formatting, and style?
- Have I corrected grammar, spelling, and usage?
- Are dialogue tags and internal thoughts clean and clear?

Tip:

This is a great place to use AI or grammar tools as support if you're used to using those types of tools—but not as a replacement for your judgment. Remember: those tools get things wrong, can insert errors and can strip your natural author voice.

And if you're prepping for a professional edit, this pass will save you money and make your editor's job easier. Run one last consistency check with a style guide if you're publishing wide.

5. Final Pass: Final Polish

Super zoom. As zoomed in as you get: proof and polish before publication, submission, querying.

Ta-da! You're so close to the end, you're ready to be D.O.N.E with these edits.

The final layer of edits is about getting the manuscript clean before you send it off, whether to your editorial team, to be published or for querying.

You're not making story changes or even really line editing changes at this stage. It's truly a nitty-gritty-details-and-leave-the-rest-alone stage.

Focus:

Polish polish polish.

This is where you handle:

- Formatting issues
- Typos
- Extra spaces
- Errant returns
- Wrong or missing punctuation
- Word mix-ups
- Minor timeline cleanup
- Name changes

- Inaccurate descriptions

If you're working with an editor, this is where a proof-reader steps in.

Ask:

- Are there lingering typos, punctuation errors, or extra spaces?
- Is everything formatted consistently (paragraphs, indents, italics, chapter headings)?
- Do name spellings, timelines, or character details still match what's in your style guide?
- Have I accidentally changed something I already fixed?
- Can I step away now without fiddling?

Tip:

Avoid the temptation to *start* with this pass! Doing so wastes effort on sections that might change entirely with your story edits.

The other thing to keep in mind? This *isn't* the rewrite stage. You already did that (or at least you should have already done that, because you're not meant to start here, remember!).

Resist the urge to fiddle fiddle fiddle and go back to the line edit level again. That's how you end up stripping your natural voice right out of the story, and you lose internal character voice consistency.

Basically, you can remove the magic of *you* if you don't let yourself let go.

THE 5-PASS EDITING METHOD WRAP-UP

Here's the good news: Just following this overview of passes will help give you enough structure to begin to focus and realize exactly where your main issues often are.

Here's the bad news: You might repeat some of these passes. You might need more than five.

The key here is to focus your attention on each pass, rather than overwhelming your brain.

What matters is editing with intention—not trying to do everything at once.

APPENDIX C: THE STARTER EDITING CHECKLIST

Use this as a jumping-off point—not a finish line.

Your editing process is unique, and this checklist is meant to guide—not dictate—your next steps. It follows a traditional editing order: big-picture content first, sentence polish last. You're going to notice some overlap between the stages.

This checklist connects directly to the 5-Pass Editing Method, and you'll use it next to help shape your personalized editing plan.

Content/Developmental/Story Edits (Pass 1 and 2)

- Compelling opening
- Main plot details
- Secondary plot details
- Pacing
- Character arc development
- Characterization

- World-building
- Representation check
- Internal/external conflict
- Deep POV
- Timeline consistency
- Relationship development/emotional progression
- Satisfying ending
- Series development

Line Edits aka Craft of Writing Edits (Pass 2 and 3)

- Sentence structure
- Clarity and flow
- Deep POV
- Filter words
- Overwriting
- Figurative language
- Description and blocking
- Dialogue (voice, purpose, realism)
- Dialogue and action tags
- Consistent tense use

Copy Edits (Pass 3 and 4)

- Name and detail consistency
- Grammar and punctuation
- Word choice (e.g., your/you're)
- Overused words or tags
- Dialogue punctuation

- Character age/descriptions
- Direct address commas
- Format of internal thoughts

Proofreading (Pass 5 but also the final pass, so may come later)

- Final grammar/spell check
- Dialogue/action tag review
- Formatting issues (headers, fonts, chapter numbering)
- Timeline or fact-check leftovers
- Style consistency
- Final read aloud or AI polish pass

APPENDIX D: STARTER AUTHOR STYLE GUIDE TEMPLATE

To purchase a comprehensive, formatted and editable
Author Style Guide Template, please visit
shop.angelajames.co

———

*The lines in this template represent either section breaks or
page breaks.*

Book/Series Title and Author Name:

Style Guide: Chicago Manual of Style (CMoS)

Dictionary: Merriam-Webster

———

NAMES

Character Names, Nicknames & Pronouns:

- Here
- Here

Real People, Celebrities, Historical Figures:

- Here
- Here

Places, Businesses, Towns, Street Names:

- Here
- Here

Brand Names & Trademarks:

- Here
- Here

———

CAPITALIZATION

Preferred Capitalization Choices:

- *Example:* Navy vs. navy.
- *Example:* Black/white when referencing race.

Sci-Fi/Fantasy Capitalized Words/Phrases:

- Made-up word
- Made-up phrase

Titles & Nicknames:

- *Example:* Do you want Duke or Queen always capitalized.
- *Example:* "I see you, sunshine." "Nobody puts Baby in the corner."

————

SPELLING

UK vs. US English Preferences:

- *Example:* grey vs. gray

Nonstandard Spellings:

- Words you don't want corrected even if spellcheck says they're wrong.

Slang, Fictional Languages, Made-Up Words:

- This duplicates slightly the above. You could decide to combine them under one heading.

————

PUNCTUATION

Oxford Comma: Yes / No

Other Punctuation Preferences:

- *Example:* Introductory comma after "oh".

————

FORMATTING

Italics:

- Non-English words: Italicized / Not italicized.
- Internal dialogue: (format preference).
- Other uses: …

Bold:

- *Example:* No bold in manuscript.
- *Example:* Always bold subheadings.

Quotation Marks:

- *Example:* Quotation marks to indicate sarcasm.
- Single quotes only within double quotation marks.

Em Dashes:

- Preference for spacing: (no spaces / spaced).

———

ALPHABETICAL QUICK REFERENCE

Use this section to track characters, names, places, specific words, phrases, or style choices alphabetically for quick reference.

A

B

C

D

E

F

G

H

I

J

K

L

M

N

O

P

Q

R

S

T

U

V

W

X

Y

Z

NOTES

Use this space for any additional style preferences or reminders:

―――――

NOTE

This style guide tracks HOW you write things (spelling, formatting, punctuation choices). For tracking WHAT you write about (character details, plot, world-building), create a separate Story Bible.

APPENDIX E: THE INCLUSIVE HEART TEST

––––––

Why are we doing this?

Maybe it's time for the Romance genre to consider making its own "test" to review the standards we're aiming for in measuring inclusion within a romance novel. It's time that we put together some standards we're looking for. Like all fiction genres, Romance has some cleanup to do for those who want the genre to be more inclusive.

How to Use

Tests to improve inclusion and representation in media are not anything new. There have been many tests, codes, and checklists in the media to work to push a set of standards. However, this appears to be the first one aimed at the romance fiction genre.

No test is fool-proof and should not be treated as such. This test, like so many others, also has limitations and will (and should be) open to criticism. Times will change and that means so will the inclusive and repre-sentative needs of the genre. This test will become outdated if it does not grow with the times.

Just like not every film passes the Bechdel test, not every romance novel will pass the Heart test. Like everything in the media, the standard will be enforced by those who feel the standard actually matters.

Warning: Not every author is aware of this test and therefore will take time for this test to circulate for romance authors to use.

Blogger/Reviewers: If you choose to use this test as a standard you'd like to communicate in your review, please note that you will need to reference the criteria in this test to your audience so the context is clear. Again, this is new, and many readers, publishers, bloggers, and authors may not be aware of this test nor abiding by these standards (though one could hope they are regardless).

Sensitivity Readers: Use this test as a guide and help point out general issues with the literary work. You can also branch off and create your own test like this which specializes in the areas you cover for sensitivity (Transphobia, Fatphobia, Islamophobia, Colorism, etc.)

Agents/Publishers/Editors: You cannot continue to profit from these harmful works yet claim to be inclusive and equitable. These areas of this test could be the minimum targets of the works you're looking to sign and/or purchase. Inclusion is not just based on what you say you won't allow, it's also what you're complicit in and what you do. It's in the products you sell---like books. Please use this test as a guiding light to discern what stories are fulfilling your inclusive brand.

The Heart Test

This is the first iteration of the Heart test and covers representation for BIPOC, femme gender, LGBTQ+, People with disabilities, and protecting racially marginalized people from harm.

This should be included in addition to a rubric scoring system. If a novel fails the HEART test, it should be flagged for further review.

Just because a book passes the Heart test doesn't mean it's a quality book, however, it is a starting point to see how much effort the author made to create an inclusive story.

First, do no harm by eliminating redemption stories for historically oppressive identities. This is not just about morality (because morality cannot be legislated) but the first rule in being inclusive is to minimize harm to the historically ignored identities. This is about allyship.

- Main characters in Romance do not hold identities aligned with the following:
    - Global or Domestic Terrorism & Hate groups
    - Genocide
    - War Crimes
    - Chattel Slavery
    - Sex Trafficking and other crimes against humanity

- BIPOC, LGBTQ+, (and intersections of such) characters (main or secondary) in Romance must have fully realized lives and dimensions, not just present as one-dimensional characters to prop up cisgender-heterosexual, white-led stories.

- BIPOC femme characters in Romance are not sexualized and not fetishized as a key character trait.

- Characters with a disability are not solely defined around their disability and are fully realized to live a happy and fulfilling life in the story. Please note that a HEA for disabled characters may resolve differently from able-bodied characters. (i.e, a character with chronic pain may still have chronic pain AND still, find love and acceptance with their partner(s).) With characters of questionable morals, even if met with comeuppance, the consequence is not tied to their disability.

- Femme main characters with questionable morals and imperfections in Romance are given a development arc without the expectation they must be perfect or free from all personality flaws.

- Black main characters in Romance should not solely operate under respectability politics, which demeans and can oppress Blackness when the character isn't exemplifying traits seen as "upstanding Black individuals" within the white gaze.

GLOSSARY

This glossary combines not only terms you'll find in the *Edit Your Way* series, but also some general publishing terms and definitions that are used regularly.

———

Accept/Reject Changes: Actions in Track Changes that allow you to finalize or discard suggested edits. Turning Track Changes on or off doesn't affect previously tracked changes—you must physically select to accept or reject them.

Accountability Partner: A person who supports and motivates you regularly in your writing and editing work, helping you maintain progress and providing feedback.

Acknowledgements: A section in a book where the author thanks those who contributed to the creation of the work.

Action Tags: Descriptions of character actions used in place of or alongside dialogue tags to convey emotion, context, blocking/movement, or deeper point of view.

Active Voice: A sentence structure where the subject performs the action.

Advanced Reader Copy (ARC): A pre-release version of a book distributed to reviewers, bloggers, and other readers for the purpose of generating early reviews and buzz. ARCs are typically sent out before full proof-reading is finished and may contain errors.

Adverbs: Words that modify verbs, adjectives, or other adverbs, explaining how, when, or how much. They are a necessary part of the English language and shouldn't be automatically eliminated from writing.

ADHD: Attention Deficit Hyperactivity Disorder; a neurodevelopmental condition that can affect focus, attention, and emotional regulation, which may impact how authors approach writing and editing tasks.

Agents: Literary agents who represent authors to publishers, helping to negotiate publishing contracts and advocate for the author's work. Authors may query agents to seek representation, and the fear of rejection from agents is a common emotional challenge in the publishing journey.

AI/Artificial Intelligence: Technology that can process and generate text, which some authors use as a tool for specific tasks like organizing information into logical bullet points or checking for potential issues in representation. While AI can help with clarity and organization, it cannot capture unique author voice or replicate authentic cadence and storytelling. AI should be used as a support tool, not a replacement for an author's own writing or judgment, as it can strip natural author voice and introduce errors.

Alpha Reader: A reader who reviews a manuscript in a very rough-draft, unedited state to give early thoughts on the story and help the author clarify choices or direction they're struggling with.

Allyship: The practice of supporting and advocating for marginalized groups. In writing, this means minimizing harm to historically ignored identities and being intentional about inclusive representation.

Author Bio: A brief description of an author's background, credentials, and other published works, used in marketing materials, book listings, PR, and more. In Angela's method, an author prepares their full (long) bio and then edits it down to a medium bio (what appears in books), a short bio (what is given to retailers, or for speaking/presenting opportunities), and a social media bio (one line that can be taken in at a glance).

Author Brand: The distinct identity, voice, and promise that an author presents to readers through their work, marketing, and public presence. Includes elements like writing style, genre focus, visual brand elements and overall professional image.

Author Platform: The combined presence and reach an author has through various channels including social media, website, newsletter, and other marketing vehicles.

Author Intrusion: When the author's personal voice, opinions, or knowledge inappropriately enter the narrative, breaking character perspective or story immersion.

Author Style Guide: A personalized reference document that tracks your specific preferences for capitalization, formatting, punctuation, and spelling across your books. It helps maintain consistency within a series or backlist and ensures everyone in your editing ecosystem is on the same page regarding your style choices.

Author Voice: The unique way an author tells stories, including their tone, style, word choices, and overall approach to storytelling.

Back Matter: The material at the end of a book after the main content, including acknowledgments, author bio, other books by the author, etc.

Backlist: Previously published books in an author's catalog. These continue to generate sales after their initial release period and can be valuable assets for ongoing revenue.

Before You Hit Send®: A long-running self-editing course created by Angela James in 2010 that has helped thousands of authors develop their editing skills. The course forms the foundation for the Edit Your Way book series and focuses on reader-focused revisions to create the best possible reading experience.

Beginning: The opening portion of your story that establishes the tone, introduces key characters, and hooks readers. It should engage readers while providing necessary context for the story ahead.

Beta Reader: A reader, often a fan, who reads and provides feedback on a manuscript before it goes through professional editing, usually in exchange for an early look at the book.

Bias: Default assumptions and prejudices that can impact how we interact with writing as editors, critique partners, and readers. These biases can allow microaggressions and potentially harmful phrasing to creep into fiction writing and other aspects of publishing.

Blocking: The description of physical movements, positions, and actions of characters within a scene. This includes how characters move through space, their gestures, and their physical interactions with their environment and other characters. Also sometimes called choreography, blocking helps readers visualize where characters are and what they're doing during scenes.

Blurb: A short promotional description of a book, typically appearing on the back cover or in online listings.

BookFunnel (bookfunnel.com): A service used to deliver digital books and promotional materials to readers.

Book Stuffing: The practice of adding excessive content to a book to artificially increase its length, often considered unethical particularly in subscription services.

Brand: see Author Brand

Brand Promise: The consistent experience and quality readers can expect from an author's work across all their books.

Brick& Mortar Store: A physical retail bookstore location. In publishing terms, this refers to when the sales team convinces a physical store to carry a book and determines in what quantities.

Call to Action: A prompt that encourages readers to take a specific action, such as signing up for a newsletter or purchasing the next book in a series.

Character Arc: The internal journey and transformation a character undergoes throughout the story, showing how they grow, change, or develop based on their experiences.

Character Voice: The distinct way a specific character

speaks, thinks, and expresses themselves, including their unique patterns of speech, word choices, and perspective.

Characterization: The way an author develops and reveals character personalities, motivations, and traits through dialogue, actions, thoughts, and narrative description.

Cliches: Overused expressions or familiar storylines that lack originality. Author voice is what separates compulsively readable stories from tired cliches.

Cliffhanger: An ending that leaves major plot points unresolved to create suspense and encourage readers to buy the next book.

Co-Writing: The practice of two or more authors collaborating to write a book together.

Conflict (External): External obstacles, challenges, or opposition that a character faces from outside forces such as other characters, society, or nature that keeps them from achieving their goal (or getting to the resolution of the book/series).

Conflict (Internal): Inner struggles, doubts, or emotional challenges that a character experiences within themselves that keep them from achieving their goal (or getting to the resolution of the book/series).

Content Edits: See Developmental Edits

Content Warning (Also called Trigger Warning): A notice at the beginning of a work alerting readers to potentially sensitive or triggering content, allowing them to make informed decisions about reading.

Copy Editing: The third stage of editing that focuses on technical accuracy, including grammar, spelling, punctuation, fact-checking, and consistency.

Copyright: Legal protection for original creative works, including written material, that grants exclusive rights to the creator.

Cover Copy: The descriptive text that appears on a book's cover or in its online listing, including the book description/blurb and author bio.

Critique Partner: A fellow writer who exchanges manuscripts with you to provide detailed feedback and suggestions for improvement.

Crowdsourcing: In editing terms, relying on too many voices or opinions when making decisions about your story. This can include using too many beta readers, asking your writing group to weigh in on every editorial suggestion, or using reviews to edit your book. Crowdsourcing can make it difficult to preserve your voice and vision because everyone reviews based on what they personally like best.

Dangling Participles: A grammatical error where a descriptive phrase doesn't clearly connect to the word it's meant to modify. Most common at the beginning of sentences, where the participle is meant to modify the subject of the sentence, but is not.

Deep Point of View (Deep POV): A narrative technique that deeply immerses readers in a character's perspective by eliminating distance between the reader and character's thoughts and experiences.

Derivative Work: A creative work based on or derived from one or more existing works.

Developmental Edits (Content Edits, Big Picture Edits): The first major stage of editing that focuses on "big picture" elements like plot, characterization, pacing, world-building, and story structure.

Dialogue: The written conversation between characters in a story, typically shown through quotation marks. This includes both what characters say aloud to each other and how they say it.

Direct Sales: Selling books directly to readers through an author's website or platform rather than through retailers.

Direct Address Comma: A comma used when directly addressing someone by name or title in dialogue or text.

Diversity: The ways in which individuals differ from each other, including but not limited to race, religion, ethnicity, gender, sexual orientation, socioeconomic status, culture, weight, disability, and physical characteristics. Diversity exists in comparison to a group, not as an individual trait.

Don't Kill the Dog: A shorthand phrase representing the importance of understanding your author brand and reader expectations. While literally about not killing beloved animal characters, it more broadly refers to avoiding story choices that might betray reader trust or break the implied promise of your genre/brand.

Draft: A version of your manuscript at any stage of completion, from first rough draft through final polished version. Different drafts reflect different stages of the writing and editing process.

Dream Sequence: A scene depicting a character's dream. Often cited as a writing "rule" to avoid, particularly as a chapter opening.

Dynamic Pricing: A pricing strategy where book prices are adjusted strategically across a series or over time to maximize sales and revenue.

EditMatch: The Complete Toolkit for Choosing the Right Editor: A resource designed to help authors identify what they need and want in an editorial partnership. It includes a workbook, checklist, and guidance for determining budget, editing goals, and finding the right editor match for your specific needs and working style.

Editor: A professional who helps improve manuscripts through various stages of editing, from developmental changes to final proofreading. Different types of editors specialize in different aspects of the editing process.

Eff the Writing "Rules": A philosophy and approach to editing that challenges the concept of absolute writing "rules". It emphasizes that while writing guidelines can be helpful, they should not be treated as unbreakable rules that override author voice or storytelling needs.

Ego: In the context of writing and editing, ego refers to the emotional attachment to one's work that can create barriers to effective editing and growth. For authors, it may manifest as resistance to editorial feedback or an unwillingness to make necessary changes.

End: The conclusion of your story that provides resolution to the main conflicts and delivers on the promises made to readers throughout the narrative.

Ereader: An electronic device designed for reading digital books, such as a Kobo, Kindle or other e-reading devices.

Etailer: An online retailer that sells ebooks and other digital products (e.g., Kobo, Amazon, Apple Books, etc.).

Equity: Refers to the ongoing process of identifying and dismantling barriers so individuals from marginalized identities can access the same opportunities and resources as others.

Fact Checking: The process of verifying the accuracy of information, details, and facts included in a manuscript.

Fast Drafting: A writing technique where the first draft is written quickly to maintain momentum, with the understanding that substantial revision will follow.

Feedback: Input, suggestions, and observations provided by editors, critique partners, beta readers, or others about your manuscript. Getting outside feedback is invaluable because we can't see what we cannot see in our own work.

Figurative Language: Literary devices that use words in non-literal ways to create vivid imagery or comparisons, including similes, metaphors, and other figures of speech.

Filter Words: Words that create distance between the reader and the character's experience (e.g., saw, heard, felt, wondered, realized).

First Person (POV): A narrative perspective where the story is told from the viewpoint of a character using "I" pronouns. Internal dialogue is written in first person, present tense.

Find/Replace: A word processing feature that allows you to search for specific text and replace it with alternative text throughout a document. Must be used carefully to avoid introducing errors.

Formatting: The process of preparing a manuscript for publication by setting consistent fonts, margins, spacing, and other visual elements according to required specifications.

Freelance/Freelancer: An independent contractor who works for multiple clients rather than being employed by a single company. In publishing, this often refers to freelance editors, cover artists, formatters, etc. who work independently rather than for a publishing house.

Front Matter: The material at the beginning of a book before the main content, including title page, copyright information, dedication, etc.

Garbage Words: A broad term referring to overused words, filler words, filter words or other words that don't add meaning to the sentence but could be removed or strengthened.

Genre Cues: Elements in cover art, blurbs, and marketing that signal to readers what genre a book belongs to.

Goal-Motivation-Conflict (GMC): What does the character want? Why do they want it? What's standing in their way of achieving/getting it?

Going Wide: Publishing books across multiple retailers rather than being exclusive to one platform.

High Concept: A unique and compelling premise that can be easily pitched and marketed.

Hook: A compelling element that draws readers in and makes them want to read more.

House Style Guide: A publisher's specific guidelines for grammar, formatting, and language usage that may differ from standard style guides.

Imposter Syndrome: Feelings of self-doubt and inadequacy despite evidence of success and competence.

Imprint (Publishing Imprint): A publisher's brand or line of books, often focused on specific genres or markets. Publishers may have multiple imprints, each with its own style guide and editorial approach. For instance, Angela James was the editorial director of Carina Press, an imprint of HarperCollins' Harlequin.

Indie Publishing: Self-publishing or independent publishing where the author maintains control over the publishing process.

Inclusion: is the intentional practice of creating environments where all people—especially those from historically excluded identities—are not only present, but have the power, opportunity, and agency to shape, participate in, and thrive within systems, organizations, and communities.

Infodump: The practice of delivering large amounts of background information, world-building details, or exposition all at once, which can overwhelm readers and slow pacing.

Internal Dialogue: A character's private thoughts or internal conversation with themselves. This is different from narrative in that it represents direct thoughts the point-of-view character has with themselves, rather than description or story progression.

Kill Your Darlings: An oft-overused or misused phrase referring to the difficult editorial decision to delete a favorite word, phrase, sentence, scene, or even character that you're particularly fond of but that doesn't serve the story.

Kindle Unlimited: Amazon's subscription service where readers can read unlimited books for a monthly fee.

Kobo Plus: Kobo's subscription service where readers can read unlimited books for a monthly fee.

Lead Magnet: A free item or bonus content offered to entice readers to join an author's newsletter or mailing list.

Line Edits: The second stage of editing that focuses on

writing craft at the sentence level, including clarity, flow and word choice.

Lived Experience: Personal, firsthand knowledge and understanding gained from actually experiencing something, particularly related to specific identities, cultures, or circumstances. Everyone brings their own lived experiences to their writing, editing, and interpretation of the book. Sensitivity readers bring their lived experiences to help ensure authentic representation in manuscripts.

Loss Leader: A book priced low or given away free to attract readers to an author's other works, typically the first book in a series.

Magic: In editing terms, refers to the transformative power of great and effective editing to elevate a story from good to great, particularly through developmental editing that enhances the reader experience.

Marketing Hook: A compelling selling point or angle used to promote a book.

Media Kit: A collection of promotional materials about an author and their books used for marketing purposes.

Metaphors: Figurative language that makes direct comparisons between two unlike things without using "like" or "as".

Microaggression: Subtle, often unintentional expressions of bias or prejudice in writing that can create harm for marginalized groups.

Microsoft Word Ribbon: The interface strip at the top of Microsoft Word that contains all the commands and features organized into tabs, providing access to the program's various tools and functions.

Narrative: The parts of the story that aren't dialogue, describing action, setting, character thoughts and feelings, and moving the story forward. Narrative can be shallow (just describing what happens) or deep (including character thoughts and feelings), but even deep narrative is distinct from internal dialogue.

Newsletter Opt-in: The process where readers sign up to receive an author's newsletter.

Othering: The behavior of emphasizing a difference from the dominant group or culture as "not us" or "less than".

Oxford Comma: The comma placed before the conjunction in a list of three or more items (e.g., "red, white, and blue"). Sometimes necessary for clarity, though its use is a style choice.

Pacing: The rhythm and speed at which your story unfolds, including how quickly or slowly events occur and information is revealed to readers.

Passive Voice: A sentence structure where the subject

receives the action rather than performing it. Not every use of "was" or "to be" is passive voice, and passive voice isn't always bad.

Pen Name (also called **Pseudonym**): An alternative name used by an author for publication, often chosen for privacy, branding, or genre distinction purposes.

Permafree: A book that is permanently available for free, usually as a marketing strategy.

Pivot: A significant change in an author's writing direction, such as switching genres or target audiences.

Plot: The sequence of events that make up your story, including the main conflict, rising action, climax, and resolution.

Point of View (POV): The perspective from which a story is told. The point of view character is the one through whose eyes and thoughts the reader experiences the story.

Pre-order: The ability for readers to purchase a book before its release date.

Price Promo: A temporary price reduction used to boost sales or visibility.

Privilege: Unearned advantages or benefits that individuals receive based on their social identities. Understanding our own privilege is crucial for recognizing why certain writing choices may be harmful and for writing inclusively. Having privilege doesn't mean you don't have hardships in your life, only that you have advantages someone without that same social identity does not.

Procrastination: Avoiding writing and editing tasks by engaging in other activities instead, such as playing games on your phone or doing household chores when you should be working on your manuscript.

Pronouns: The words used to refer to people without using their names (such as he, she, they). In character development, it's important to track what pronouns each character uses.

Proofread: The final stage of editing that focuses on catching any remaining errors in spelling, punctuation, formatting, and presentation.

Publishers: Companies that produce and distribute books.

Query/Querying: The process of pitching your manuscript to literary agents or publishers, typically through a query letter.

Quick Access Toolbar: A customizable bar in Microsoft Word that provides one-click access to frequently used commands and features.

Quick Win: An editing task that's relatively easy to

accomplish and provides immediate satisfaction or visible improvement to your manuscript. While valuable for maintaining momentum, quick wins should not be used to avoid more substantial developmental editing work.

Rapid Release: A publishing strategy where books (often in a series) are released in quick succession to maintain reader interest and momentum.

Reader Experience: How readers engage with, understand, and emotionally connect with your story. This encompasses everything from the ease of following the plot to the emotional impact of character arcs. While writing may be for yourself, editing should focus on optimizing the reader's experience.

Relationship Development: How connections between characters evolve throughout the story, whether romantic, familial, or friendship-based.

Representation: The inclusion and portrayal of diverse identities, experiences, and perspectives in writing. A thorough edit should examine representation to ensure authentic, respectful portrayals and to identify potential bias, microaggressions, or stereotypes.

Return on Investment (ROI): The measure of profit or benefit gained compared to the resources invested.

Revise and Resubmit (R&R): When an editor or agent

requests specific revisions to a manuscript before making a final decision.

Rough Draft: An early version of your manuscript, typically the first complete draft before any significant editing has occurred.

Second Person (POV): A narrative perspective where the story addresses the reader directly using "you" pronouns.

Secondary Characters: Supporting characters who play significant roles in the story but are not the main protagonist(s).

Self-Edits: The process of reviewing and revising your own work before sending it to professional editors or publishing. Includes multiple stages from developmental editing through proofreading.

Sell-through Rate: The percentage of readers who continue buying books in a series after reading the first book. A measure of reader retention.

Sensitivity Reader: A reader who reviews manuscript content specifically for accurate and respectful representation of certain identities, cultures, or experiences.

Sentence Structure: The way sentences are constructed, including word order, length, and grammatical patterns. Sentence structure contributes to author voice and affects the rhythm and flow of writing.

Series: Multiple books connected by characters, world, or theme, requiring additional attention to consistency and continuity during editing.

Series Bible: A document tracking important details, characters, and plot points across a series to maintain consistency.

Series Style Guide: see Style Guide

Similes: Figurative language that makes comparisons using "like" or "as".

Street Team: A group of dedicated readers who help promote an author's books.

Show vs. Tell: A writing concept referring to the difference between describing what happens (telling) and allowing readers to experience it through action, dialogue, and sensory details (showing).

Showing: In writing, demonstrating concepts or providing examples rather than just explaining them. In critique, showing means providing one example of what you mean rather than rewriting entire sections.

Story Arc: The overall shape of your narrative from beginning to end, including the rising action, climax, and resolution.

Story Structure: The overall organization and framework of a narrative, including how events are arranged and how the story unfolds from beginning to end.

Style Guide: A document that establishes consistent guidelines for formatting, spelling, punctuation, and other writing conventions.

Subrights: Subsidiary rights; additional rights to a work beyond the primary publication rights, which may include audio, translation, film, or other adaptations.

Super Fan: A highly engaged reader who consistently buys an author's books and promotes them to others.

Suspense Elements: Techniques used to create tension and keep readers engaged, including foreshadowing, withholding information, and creating anticipation.

Target Audience: The specific group of readers most likely to be interested in and purchase a book.

Tech Stack: The collection of software tools and platforms an author uses to run their publishing business.

Telling: In narrative writing, directly stating information rather than showing it through action, dialogue, or sensory details. While often contrasted with showing, telling has its place in effective storytelling

Tense: The time frame in which a story is told, such as

past tense or present tense. Maintaining consistent tense use throughout a manuscript is important for clarity.

Tertiary Characters: Minor characters who appear briefly or have very small roles in the story, beyond the main and secondary characters.

Third person (POV): A narrative perspective where the story is told about characters using "he," "she," or "they" pronouns rather than "I."

Timeline: The chronological sequence of events in your story, which needs to remain consistent and logical throughout.

TL;DR: Stands for "Too Long; Didn't Read". A brief summary at the beginning of a chapter or section that provides the key points for readers who want a quick overview.

Toxic Positivity: False or excessive positivity that dismisses genuine concerns or negative emotions. In contrast, intentional, real positive support acknowledges difficulties while providing meaningful encouragement.

Track Changes: A word processing feature that records all edits made to a document, allowing authors and editors to see and review changes.

Trademark: A legally protected word, phrase, symbol,

or design that identifies and distinguishes a brand or product, such as *Before You Hit Send*® and Book Boss®.

Traditional Publishing: Publishing through established publishing houses that handle editing, production, and distribution.

Translations: Editions of a book in languages other than the one it was written in, adapted by professional book translators or fans.

Trigger Warning: A notice about potentially traumatic content in a book, allowing readers to make informed choices about their reading.

Typographical Errors: Mistakes in typing, spelling, or formatting in a manuscript; commonly called typos.

Universal Fantasy: A book concept with broad appeal that can resonate with many readers.

Virtual Assistant (VA): A contractor who helps with various publishing tasks remotely.

Visual Pacing Technique: A method for evaluating and adjusting the rhythm and flow of your writing by examining the visual appearance of text on the page, including paragraph length, white space, and dialogue distribution.

Voice (Author): The unique way an author tells stories, including tone, style, word choices, sentence structure, and overall approach to storytelling. Author voice is what separates compulsively readable stories from tired cliches and familiar storylines, and it's one of the keystones of creating reader fans.

Voice (Character): The distinct way a specific character speaks, thinks, and expresses themselves, including their unique patterns of speech, word choices, accent, dialect, and perspective. Character voice should be different from the author's voice and distinct from other characters' voices.

White as Default: The unconscious practice of only describing characters' physical characteristics when they are not white, thereby treating whiteness as the assumed norm.

Wide Publishing: Distribution of books across multiple retailers rather than exclusive distribution through a single platform.

Wins: The positive achievements and successes in your writing and editing process, from small accomplishments to major milestones. Tracking wins is an important emotional support practice during editing, helping maintain motivation and confidence.

Work in Progress (WIP): A manuscript that is currently being written or edited; an unfinished work.

Word Processing Program: Software designed for creating, editing, formatting, and printing text documents.

Common examples include Microsoft Word, Google Docs, and Apple Pages.

World-building: The creation and development of the setting, including its physical, cultural, and social elements, whether realistic or fantastic.

Writing to Market: Creating books specifically targeted to current market demands and reader preferences.

Writer's Block: The experience of being unable to write or make progress on a manuscript, often due to creative, emotional, or psychological barriers.

Writing Rules: Common writing advice often presented as absolute requirements but which should be treated as flexible guidelines that can be adapted or broken based on author voice and story needs.

ABOUT THE AUTHOR

In true meta fashion, I'll tell you that I forgot to include this page. Then I remembered I forgot. And when making some additions before proofreading, I forgot again. And, honestly, this should have been the easiest part because I have about 4 different bios that I use all the time. So it was already written, I just needed to copy and paste and make some small revisions.

Plus, I think this book has told you more about *who* I am than any bio ever could, but here we go...

———

Hi, I'm Angela James.

With over two decades in publishing—including directing two major imprints and editing more than 1,000 titles (several hitting #1 on the *New York Times* bestseller list)—I've built my career on understanding what makes books succeed. Now, as a bestselling indie editor and an author career coach, I'm putting that expertise to work for authors like you, who may not want to work within the traditional publishing setting (though I do also still edit for a few trad pubs!)

I've been featured in *Fast Company* as a digital trailblazer, along with *Wired* and *The Washington Post* for my publishing acumen, but what drives me, what's *always* driven me, is making publishing achievable.

That's why I originally created *Before You Hit Send®*, why I wrote this book, and why I developed products and communities that help you move past the hustle and burnout that publishing is sometimes known for, and instead toward strategies (and mindsets) that deliver results and success on *your* terms.

I work with both fiction authors building sustainable careers as well as those authors and experts who want to write nonfiction and share their knowledge in book form. When we work together, I'm not offering generic advice—you're getting what *you* need, tailored to you.

Alongside all that, I'm an animal lover, a frequent concertgoer across many different genres of music, I'm always thinking about my next tattoo, and I firmly believe that, yes, pineapple does belong on pizza.

But most of all, I love books. Books really do define so much of my life, and it's one of the biggest joys of my life to help authors bring their books to reality.

To find out more about my services, visit my website at angelajames.co or join my newsletter.

Follow me on social media

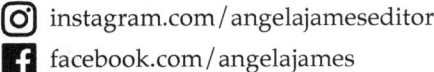

instagram.com/angelajameseditor
facebook.com/angelajames